WHAT HAPPENED TO BELÉN

THE UNJUST IMPRISONMENT

THAT SPARKED A

WOMEN'S RIGHTS MOVEMENT

HarperOne
An Imprint of HarperCollins*Publishers*

WHAT HAPPENED TO BELÉN

ANA ELENA CORREA

TRANSLATED FROM THE SPANISH BY JULIA SANCHES

✳ FOREWORD BY MARGARET ATWOOD ✳

HarperCollins books may be purchased for educational, business, or sales promotional use. For information, please email the Special Markets Department at SPsales@harpercollins.com.

Originally published as *Somos Belén* in Argentina in 2019 by Grupo Editorial Planeta.

FIRST HARPERONE EDITION PUBLISHED IN 2024

Designed by Yvonne Chan
Illustration by Camila Rosa

Library of Congress Cataloging-in-Publication Data has been applied for.

ISBN 978-0-06-331673-7

24 25 26 27 28 LBC 5 4 3 2 1

For Belén

For Malena and Felipe

I would venture to guess that Anon, who wrote so many poems without signing them, was often a woman.

—VIRGINIA WOOLF, *A ROOM OF ONE'S OWN*

CONTENTS

FOREWORD
BY MARGARET ATWOOD

I'm Margaret Atwood, the author of *The Handmaid's Tale* and its sequel, *The Testaments*. This novel's live launch worked with Equality Now to inform a wider audience about the challenges facing women's rights worldwide.

Equality Now is an international organization that labors to change restrictive, unfair, and sometimes lethal laws governing women and girls. Their *Testaments*-related campaign is titled "Gilead Is a Global Reality." It outlines the many instances—from sexual violence to lack of reproductive rights and protections to exclusion from education—in which the practices and laws in the fictional Republic of Gilead mirror those in real states. This is not surprising, because the details in my two books featuring Gilead, as well as those in the television series, came from reality in the first place.

As Equality Now knows too well, the story of Belén is not an isolated miscarriage of justice. Being jailed for having had an abortion when, in fact, you've had a miscarriage—this plotline could have come right out of the pages of *Gilead*. So could an incident that happened earlier in 2019, when a woman who lost her baby because another woman shot her in the stomach was then charged with manslaughter for endangering the baby by getting into a fight. Alabama thought better of this travesty, but the laws there enabled such a ridiculous charge. In some parts of the United States—a country viewed so long during the Cold War by many others as a bastion of freedom, democracy, and fairness—laws specific to women are hurtling backward as fast as the lawmakers can manage. Not incidentally, the removal or denial of women's right to equality and fairness has been a feature of every totalitarian regime I can remember.

* * *

Here are a couple of things I've been pondering:

1. Democracy depends on the idea that government is based on the consent of the governed. But in the case of women and girls of reproductive age, this has never been the case. Why not? Because this population segment is always in the minority; it's outnumbered by men and by women who are no longer of reproductive age. So the laws about women's fertile bodies are always controlled by people who are not fertile women. If these laws were based on the consent of the governed, only those subject to them would be allowed to vote on them.

2. Restrictive reproductive laws that force women and girls to give birth unwillingly to infants they can't afford, or to retain fetuses that may kill them, or to carry dead babies until they abort spontaneously, are instances of the state requisitioning citizens' bodies for state purposes, whatever those purposes may be called. The equivalent for men is conscription into the army. But even though you may not wish to be in the army, once you are in, your food, clothing, lodging, and medical care are covered by the taxpayer. Has any state offered to supply similar goods and services to women and girls pregnant against their wills? Not to my knowledge. They want to force women to give birth and also to incur the expense of pre-natal and post-natal care. If states are serious about the ownership of women's bodies and about forcing women to give birth

against their wills, they ought to pay for this imposed service. Gilead does.

3. Could it be that the criminalization of reproductive-rights practices is a profit-making scheme? In what places are there prisons-for-profit? Is there a correlation between this form of quasi slavery and restricted reproductive rights? I'd be interested to find out.

* * *

In Argentina—which provided some of the real-life practices embedded in *The Handmaid's Tale*, notably the baby stealing carried out under the generals—Belén's plight had a spotlight shone upon it, forcing a review and ultimately an acquittal. But this happened only after years of suffering on Belén's part, and then only due to a massive protest against the denial of proper due process to this woman by a group of activists determined to reverse this instance of bad justice. (In this way, at least, Argentina is not Gilead: Gilead would not tolerate such a protest.)

* * *

How many other Beléns are there in the world? How many women have died because they were afraid to go to a hospital while miscarrying, terrified that they would be charged with murder? How would we know? As so often when it comes to women, injustices are hidden from view, buried in silence and euphemism. We owe a debt of gratitude to those who uncovered this one injustice, at least.

1

STATION STORIES

In train stations, there are many people hiding stories we aren't always prepared to hear.

A woman in her thirties is at a clothing stall in the Constitución neighborhood of Buenos Aires. She wears her long, straight hair tied back and a pink bandana around her neck. April sales have been slow because of the economic crisis, freeing her up to watch the congressional debate about legalizing abortion on her cell phone. When Soledad Deza starts talking about the Belén case, she turns up the volume.

"I live in Tucumán. I'm a lawyer and a feminist from the province where Belén was imprisoned for twenty-nine months for abortion after she miscarried in a hospital. Later, the women's movement helped free her." Marina, the salesperson in the next stall, is listening and says:

"I didn't realize that had happened in your province. Poor girl. Did you know her?"

"No. Big place and all," replies the young woman, who has started going by her real name again—the one she was arrested under about four years ago—after moving to Buenos Aires. Here in Buenos Aires, no one knows she is Belén.

The woman is waiting for her shift to end so she can meet her lawyer, Soledad, who has brought her a copy of the final disposition issued by the Supreme Court of Tucumán, exonerating her of the charges for which she spent two years in prison in the outskirts of San Miguel de Tucumán. Belén needs this document because, according to the National Registry of Recurrence, she still has a criminal record. If she doesn't get it expunged, Belén may have a hard time finding a better job.

Around that time of the afternoon, in the same room in Congress where Soledad spoke earlier that day, abortion opponents now take the stand. The lawyer Máximo Fonrouge, president of the Buenos Aires bar association, underscores the rights of flora and fauna to be protected, extending to embryos the same rights as trees and animals. He also mentions hedonistic temptation.

Soledad is waiting for her on the corner of Avenida Callao and Avenida Rivadavia, outside the Congressional Palace. If there's one thing Belén doesn't like about this city, it's crowds, but she enjoys seeing girls sporting green bandanas and glitter. When she meets Soledad, some women walking beside her stop to say hello.

"Did they recognize me? I'm not ready for people to know who I am yet."

Soledad laughs and tells her to relax.

"No, sweetie. They're saying hello to you because we're all happy and we're all saying hello."

The other women congratulate Soledad for her presentation in Congress. They also mention the speech that the author Claudia Piñeiro gave before her. Belén stays quiet, listening. Several of them are talking about her case.

Soledad moves away from the group and says, with a big smile:

"Listen, sweetie, the reason abortion rights are on the table right now is in part thanks to you. Your case made it possible for abortion to be debated in Argentina."

Then they immediately snap a selfie with the final disposition, a picture neither of them will upload to social media but that they both save to their cell phones.

Belén doesn't stay long. She doesn't want to miss her train to Lomas de Zamora, the Buenos Aires suburb where she's been living for the past two years.

It's getting chilly. On the platform, her phone dings with a message from her boyfriend:

"Let me know when you're close and I'll come meet you at the station. I made guiso de arroz."

The date is April 12, 2018.

2

AN ORDINARY WOMAN

The Supreme Court of Tucumán ordered Belén's release in August 2016, almost three years into her prison term. This was only possible thanks to Soledad Deza, the Tucumán-based lawyer who took on her case after finding out by chance three months earlier that a woman had been imprisoned for a miscarriage. The woman had been sentenced to eight years for homicide aggravated by the closeness of the perpetrator's relationship to the victim. Six months later, the same Supreme Court acquitted Belén.

Since Belén's release, almost no one who followed her case knows where she is. She is cited in abortion debates, and a brief statement she made was featured in a documentary. But a part of her story remains unknown.

Belén has shared her whereabouts only with her family and a small group of people who supported her throughout her trial and subsequent release. One of these people is Soledad Deza.

There is a story here that needs to be told. I need to know what happened to Belén, what happened in the province where she was sentenced, and what happened to the women who helped set her free.

With this in mind, I begin to write about a case that only a handful of people who live in the very country where it unfolded still remember. Because no one was talking about abortion back in 2016, and because there was never a face for them to accuse or defend. Only a name: Belén. And a lot of questions.

Why does she insist on remaining anonymous? How did a miscarriage land her in pretrial detention for close to three years? Why did her case have greater impact internationally than in the country where it occurred? How did she go from a murder conviction to a full acquittal? Where is Belén?

In two of the handful of interviews Belén gave while in prison and following her exoneration, she mentioned wanting to write a book about her experiences.

"So that people will realize I'm just an ordinary woman, not a murderer, not the monster I've been made out to be."

3

SOLEDAD

Like a story written in reverse, I remember the day Belén was released and her lawyer's explanation for why she was unjustly imprisoned.

Unlike God, who is said to serve in the capital, Soledad Deza practices law in San Miguel de Tucumán. It isn't easy to find a moment for the two of us to talk. When Soledad isn't teaching or leading workshops, she's counseling women on issues of gender-based violence or cases in which their reproductive rights were disrespected. It's December when I decide to write this book, and my sense of urgency has to adjust to reality. Another woman has been unjustly detained, and for a week Soledad's life is once more on hold. Her friend Larisa Moris, with whom she shares a teaching load and a law practice, has asked for Soledad's help with one of her students' mothers. The mother had hurt her partner in self-defense. Now she is under arrest while he is free. And Cecilia, Larisa's student, wants her mother to be able to attend her graduation. There's no time to lose.

Soledad doesn't sleep. She sweeps the city for evidence and contacts. She files claims.

The woman is released a week later, and although she didn't get to put on the dress they'd bought for her to wear at Cecilia's graduation, at least her daughter was able to attend her own dinner.

This is what Soledad's life, and that of the women around her, is like.

Fundación Mujeres x Mujeres (the Women for Women Foundation), of which Soledad is president, is located on the first floor of a low building in a central Tucumán neighborhood. The first thing you see when you step inside is the image of a woman bending her arm with her hand in a fist and the words WE CAN DO IT. The rest of the decor consists of regional artifacts, a lot of color, and framed news clippings and photos of protestors demanding Belén's release. The mask Belén wore the day she was set free sits on Soledad's desk.

Soledad is short and slender. The smile on her face telegraphs her kindness and a great sense of humor, which seems to be another one of her weapons.

I start by asking about her past. I want to know when she decided to become the keeper of justice for women. Was it in high school, maybe? Something in her family history? As if there were some magical moment when a person transforms into something else, as if some multicausal behavior or flash of epiphany could turn someone into a superhero or heroine. Soledad challenges my hypothesis. She tells me she went to a traditional school in Tucumán, "but see, I was in the rugby club. I was honestly a bit shallow." She graduated in law from the National University of Tucumán and started a legal firm with a colleague.

Eventually, the two partners dissolved their legal practice due to disagreements over their views on gender issues.

And when did she begin advocating for women's rights? "Nothing unusual there, either. I wanted to do a postdoc in Buenos Aires, so I started looking into my options. In the end, I had to choose between two master's programs. I chose the one on gender studies at the Latin American Faculty of Social Sciences. But I could've gone for something else. That's where my interest in gender issues began. And kept growing."

I get the sense she's holding back. Taking on a case like Belén's the way she did, and in a province like Tucumán, can't just be chalked up to a master's program in Buenos Aires. Or maybe it can, but I keep pushing.

"Something happened, and it made me swear I would never let anyone else go through what I did. I had an illegal abortion. The whole thing took me by surprise. This can happen to any woman. My dad's a well-known doctor, a university professor. He was traveling at the time. So I went to the kind of place where no one on earth would feel safe. You can imagine what it was like. Suddenly, I was experiencing illegality and its many consequences. The moment when you feel you've lost your autonomy, then all your rights, all of them, are suspended. I've never talked about it, you know? But my kids are all grown-up now. That experience was a huge motivator. Why are women put through that? If it was awful for me, then what must it be like for women who don't have the resources? Something inside me woke up. I might never get any rest, but I would do something for women's rights. No one deserves to be treated that way."

She starts telling me how she found out about Belén's case. I ask her to check if Belén would agree to see me.

A week later I get a WhatsApp message from Soledad.

"I spoke to Belén. She has your number. She's going to get in touch in a few days. She's happy to talk. Good luck with the book!"

4

HI, IT'S ME, BELÉN

I finally set off to meet the protagonist of our story. Belén still uses a pseudonym to communicate with strangers. Although the people in her past and her present know her by her real name, they don't always know she is Belén.

I receive a WhatsApp message that says: "Hi, Ana. It's me, Belén." I'd wanted to hug her for so long. Now I finally get to see her face. She's beautiful. I don't know how I'd imagined her looking before, but from then on I put a face to every minute Belén lived through until the moment she set foot in the hospital. I'm not sure how to add her to my contacts. Should I use her real name as a decoy or another pseudonym altogether? I do what feels most logical. I save her in WhatsApp as Belén. This is how she introduced herself to me. This is how we came to know her. This is how she still wants to be known.

We agree to meet at her workplace. When most people are on holiday for carnival, Belén is working twelve-hour shifts at the clothing stall. It's sweltering. The twists and turns of life: I take the same bus line as I did the first time I left the house after recovering from abortion-induced PTSD. Number 12. And I get off at the same stop where I sent a text message that said: "I'm so happy. I managed to ride the bus. This is freedom."

There are a ton of clothing stalls at the street corner Belén mentioned: men's, women's, and children's apparel. I can't see her. I shoot her a text, and she tells me there's an orange dress hanging at the entrance.

I finally find the orange dress and her standing next to it. Even though we recognize each other by sight, I wait until I'm within arm's reach before quietly asking if she is Belén. She says yes. We hug.

I've brought her a book as a present. I'd wanted to get her a copy of Virginia Woolf's *A Room of One's Own* but hadn't been able to find it, so instead I give her *Good Night Stories for Rebel Girls*. Later I would learn she preferred novels and poetry.

She tells me about her past few months in Buenos Aires. About some of her disappointments. She doesn't want to be pressured into revealing her real identity.

Soon after, I head out to get us a snack. Croissants and churros. She likes churros best.

"You have no idea how crazy I am about these things. The prison inspectors confiscated them because they were scared people would smuggle in drugs or weapons. By the end, they'd eased up a bit and started letting me eat a couple of churros. I was lucky. Some women were really nice to me in prison.

"Soledad mentioned you want to write a book. Tell me about it. I like the idea. I just don't want anyone harassing my family. Can you believe they're still being harassed? They've been through enough."

I ask her about the book she's writing.

"I filled four whole notebooks with everything I've lived through. One Sunday when I was alone at home I went into the backyard and burned them one by one. I wanted all the suffering I'd experienced throughout those three years in prison to go up in smoke. I hoped it would help me burn that past and move on."

5

ALFEÑIQUES AND HAMBURGERS

I had a job lined up when I moved here from Tucumán. At a textile-printing factory. I love design and used to make clothes for a living, both in prison and after I was released. But the factory closed a few months after I got here. Then I took every job under the sun at the train station. I was a waitress, a salesperson at a couple of clothing stalls. But then at one point I wound up needing health insurance, so when the manager of a cleaning business offered me a job I said yes. It wasn't a great job, but at least I got paid every month. Then one of the other employees started disrespecting me. I won't take abuse ever again. So I quit, and since everyone around here knows me, they offered me a job at this stall. I like the clothes, but they don't sell. I don't know what's going to happen.

I really wanted to go to the National Women's Conference last year, but it was too far away. This year I found out it's taking place in La Plata, and I'd like to attend. Will you come with me? We could go with Soledad.

The thing I most miss about Tucumán is my family. I dream of getting to hug my mother again, my sister and nieces. I haven't seen my mom since I left Tucumán. Another thing I miss are alfeñiques, those chewy sweets made with molasses, and molasses alfajores. If you ever go to Tucumán, you have to try a real milanesa sandwich. They're nothing like the ones you get here. The sandwiches are huge and the lettuce is sliced really thin. They're delicious.

The thing I don't miss is people talking about things they know nothing about. Since moving here there have been dozens of times when I was convinced I wouldn't get ahead, but whenever that happened my boyfriend would say, "You can do it, you've been through a lot worse, of course you can do it."

I hadn't seen him since high school. When he heard what happened to me, he reached out to my family and said he wanted to see me. I didn't want him visiting me in prison. I didn't like anyone visiting me in prison. Can you imagine? No one enjoys being locked up. Then, people who see you there might just think you're a criminal. That's why I didn't want him to come visit.

My favorite thing about Buenos Aires? You're going to laugh. The hamburgers. Sometimes I go all the way from my house [in Lomas de Zamora] to Constitución just to eat a delicious hamburger from this one restaurant. In prison we never got hamburgers.

6

I'LL HELP IN ANY WAY I CAN

"Did I tell you I was in a documentary? I just heard it's going to be screened at Cannes. It was really hard to say yes, but I want to help in any way I can. The one thing I asked them was not to show my face or my name."

It's a freezing cold May day in Buenos Aires in 2019 when Juan Solanas's *Let It Be Law* is screened at the Cannes festival. International media is talking about the Belén case again. Along with the story of Ana Acevedo—a young woman who died after being denied access to a legal abortion and therefore the chemotherapy she needed to treat her cancer—Belén's is one of the most influential.

That same day, Belén decides she wants to buy a blanket because hers burned in a small fire at her house.

"See you tomorrow? Besides buying a blanket, I'd like to visit El Rosedal park."

Belén is invited to a private screening of the film at the Library of Congress a month later. It's being held for the representatives who helped draft the new bill, people involved in the National Campaign for Legal, Safe, and Free Abortion in Argentina (which we'll call the National Campaign for Abortion), and anyone who took part in some way. Belén asks me to go with her. Just a few hours before the screening, she calls to say she isn't feeling well and can't make it. She wants me to attend and tell her about it.

It's a good documentary. It shows a part of the story a lot of people are in denial about: the fact that illegal abortions primarily affect women who are poor. In the movie, Belén is in shadow and her face isn't visible, per her request. All we get is her voice, which takes the form of a desperate cry.

Most of the women interviewed in the documentary, which delves into the underworld of clandestine abortions, appear again at the end of film when they say with a smile: "Let it be law."

But Belén doesn't. Her silhouette in the dark, her voice, her pain, and her story are all she agreed to share. And it's plenty. But the bright side of her is missing. She's more than her experiences, more than that cry. I mull it over, talk to her and then to Victoria Solanas, the film's executive producer. Maybe that's the first step: her saying on the big screen, "Don't forget what I was put through." The time for her to tell the whole story will eventually come.

7

THE REAL STORY

It's been five months since our first meeting. Across conversations in El Rosedal, on the phone, in the train station, and through numerous interviews and archival visits, we've reconstructed her story. It's a holiday, just as it was the first time we met. I'm reminded of what Belén said to me that day, about how she burned everything she had written.

"Are you sure you want this book to be published?"

"Yes, I think I need help closing this chapter, so I can leave behind the worst thing that ever happened to me. I need someone to speak out about what actually happened. I left Tucumán because the press kept saying all kinds of things about me. Doing horrible things. They broadcast a picture of a dead fetus next to my file on TV. They said whatever popped into their minds. I didn't want my name getting out, and they released it anyway. Are you going to publish my real name?"

"Of course not," I reply.

"Some people called to look into me, wanting to know if I'd experienced gender-based violence, if my family was responsible for anything. I don't know where they get these ideas from. Don't they realize how awful it was for me? It's like they want to make up news about me, as if what they've already made up isn't enough.

"Yes, I want you to write the book. I want you to use my voice to tell the story."

8

THOSE WHO STAY AND THOSE WHO GO

"When I was a kid, I wanted to figure skate and be a kindergarten teacher," Belén tells me.

But she couldn't. She was lucky to get through most of high school, the first in her family. She had two incompletes, in social work and public opinion. On the day of finals, she got peritonitis, a swelling in the lining of her belly and abdomen.

"Just as I was about to take my finals, I got peritonitis. My highest grade was in culture. That's the class where I started feeling bad. I told the teacher to stop moving so much because it was making me dizzy. Then he realized I wasn't well. I turned yellow and my blood pressure dropped," Belén says.

"The high school principal called my mom and told her I was pregnant. He was sure of it. My mom kept saying no. Meanwhile, I could barely talk. She insisted on calling an ambulance while the principal told her, 'Listen, all the girls here end up pregnant.' When my mom gets an idea in her head, nothing can stop her. The ambulance arrived, and the doctor said I needed emergency surgery. They told my mom it was a good thing she called immediately. One more day, and I might not have lived to tell the tale."

In 2016, at the age of twenty-five, Belén dreams of going back to school. Even though she's been seeing someone for two years, she isn't thinking about marriage. On weekends she goes to Parque 9 de Julio, a massive green space with a sampling of all of Tucumán's lush plant life. She skates around in a pair of secondhand rollerblades she got from the market.

As with many provinces in Argentina, the social inequality in Tucumán is stark. It's where a rural guerrilla militia was first formed, as well as Operativo Independencia, the cornerstone of what would become the armed forces' plan to systematically disappear and execute political dissidents, first by decree of a constitutional government and later through the establishment of a military dictatorship that began on March 24, 1976, and lasted until 1983. In those years, the province was devastated by military control.

Its airs as the so-called Garden of the Republic and the intellectualism enshrined in the National University of Tucumán contrast with another of the region's main characteristics: it is one of the most backward places in the country for the protection of women's rights. It is also the only province to have reelected a man who served as its governor during the military dictatorship. A province that the Nazi war criminal Adolf Eichmann temporarily called home and from which important figures such as the musician Mercedes Sosa and the novelist Tomás Eloy Martínez were forced to flee. A province that produced progressive leaders who could not govern in their own hometown but could in a place like Canada, like the current minister of transport, Pablo Rodriguez; or Gerardo Pisarello, a member of the Congress of Deputies in Spain as well as the left-wing party Podemos, and the son of radical leader Ángel

Pisarello, who was kidnapped and disappeared during the military dictatorship.

The only people left in Tucumán are the ones who stayed behind: those who fought, those who were not expelled, those who won, and those who lost but have yet to lose everything.

Belén lives in Las Talitas, a neighborhood abutting San Miguel de Tucumán, the region's capital city. The neighborhood grew so much that in 1986 it was designated as a municipality and now forms part of what is known as Gran Tucumán. "Gran," or "Greater," is a euphemism for the sprawl surrounding big cities across Argentina, such as Gran Buenos Aires, Gran Rosario, and Gran Córdoba, setting them apart from the city proper. The people who live there generally work in the city center and are on the front line of every crisis and mass layoff. Not all of them are alike. Gran Tucumán, for example, is incredibly hot.

The gray of Las Talitas contrasts with the lush green of the rest of the province. Tafí del Valle is without a doubt one of the most stunning places in Argentina. Less marketed than the Salta region of the Calchaquí Valleys, it exudes beauty, nature, and magic. This is where Belén went on her high school graduation trip. It was a different time.

Belén works Mondays to Fridays at a cooperative contracted by the city's Ministry of Social Development. What little she makes she puts toward helping out in the house where she lives with her mother, father, and three of six siblings, and toward her savings, since she still hasn't given up on the idea of going back to school. Everyone told her that the best she could do was study to work in corrections. But Belén likes children.

9

STOMACH PAIN

"I've always had a big appetite. I'm hopeless against sugarcane sweets, they're so delicious. Ever since I was little my mom has always said, 'You'll get a stomachache if you go on eating like that.' And she was right a lot of the time. So the first thing I thought that night was that I'd overdone it, or that I needed surgery."

The year is 2014. A Friday in March, when the difference between the heat of day and the relief of night grows sharper. It's the first day of fall, and Belén has terrible abdominal pain. She doesn't say anything at work because she doesn't like leaving early or calling attention to herself. She asks around the office for painkillers, but none of her co-workers has any. At seven in the evening she walks to the bus stop, doubled over in pain. When she gets home, she tells her mom she isn't feeling well and lies down in the bedroom she shares with two of her sisters. It doesn't help. The pangs in her belly are getting worse.

After the bout of peritonitis that kept her from finishing high school, Belén suffered complications and had to undergo surgery. This is why she and her family are now in a panic, convinced this is another complication.

She asks her mom to go to the hospital with her. Her mom tells her to rest a while longer, hoping it will pass. Try as she might, Belén can't relax. The pangs are now cramps. At three in the morning, she can't bear it anymore. They decide to go to the hospital.

"I can't walk," Belén tells her mom.

The only way she is going to make it to the hospital is by taxi. She doesn't know if it's the pain or an unseasonable chill in the air, but she feels cold, so she puts on her favorite jacket, the only one that's actually hers and not a hand-me-down from one of her siblings: a white Adidas with little flowers on it.

As in many other parts of the world, there are two kinds of hospitals in Tucumán. The clean ones with plenty of doctors and nurses to attend to patients, a clear view through the windows, labs, X-ray machines, ultrasound devices, gauze, and emotional support. And then there are the other hospitals, where people like Belén go.

Belén and her mother arrive at the Hospital de Clínicas Dr. Nicolás Avellaneda in the Villa Urquiza neighborhood after three thirty a.m. They don't stop to look at the massive structure that rises like a mirror or fortress across from the hospital, dwarfed by its presence. The largest men's prison in Tucumán. Everyone who goes to the Avellaneda hospital is used to it. Although the building was recently remodeled, it still looks old and neglected. When they walk into the emergency room, they are not checked in by any clerical staff, let alone any nurses.

Instead two police officers handle her admission. They take her name and tell her to sit in the waiting room. When it's her turn to be seen by the doctor on duty, a police officer is also the one who calls her forward.

According to the emergency room's records, on March 21, sometime between three thirty and four a.m., a woman—twenty-five years old and single—was admitted with abdominal pain. It was presumed to be a gastrointestinal issue.

They conduct a cursory checkup. Sending for an ultrasound for acute pain is out of the question. In hospitals like Avellaneda, the medical staff do not treat causes but symptoms, so they give her an injection for the pain and leave her lying on a cot.

The first doctor who sees her jots down "acute abdomen." He notes: "Previous history of peritonitis, possible complications."

FROM CRAMPS TO HOMICIDE

Because she looks quite frail and they still don't know if her gut integrity is compromised, they give her IV fluids. While she is waiting, she goes to the bathroom for the second time, down the long hallway. She sees a small amount of blood, a clot. She's a little frightened, but feels so unwell that she heads straight back to her cot. A nurse pulls a blanket over her to keep her warm. About an hour later she suddenly says to her mother:

"I think I peed myself."

It isn't pee. Before long, the bleeding has turned into hemorrhaging. The nurse sees the blood and begins to suspect the patient doesn't have a case of acute abdomen at all; she calls the doctor back. The sun is just rising when Belén is taken up to the first floor of the hospital.

The doctor who sees her in the gynecology ward is José Martín. He examines Belén and explains that what she just experienced was a miscarriage, then jots this down in her medical record. He tells her he will have to conduct a D&C, a dilation and curettage. In other words, he will have to scrape her uterine lining. Belén is shocked.

What do you mean pregnant? What are they saying?

She doesn't have time to react. The medical staff leave to get the operating room ready. Right when they're about to take her there, right when she wants to ask them what they're going to do to her, a policewoman barges onto the floor screaming. Amid all the confusion, Belén hears the officer ask if any patients had been admitted with hemorrhaging—a fetus had just been found in the bathroom at the other end of the hospital. The doctor doesn't hesitate before handing her Belén's medical record.

They wheel her to the operating room in tears. She is exhausted and in pain. She is also afraid. The policewoman looks at her lying in the cot and pens the word "homicide" in her medical record as she leaves the room.

CORPORAL CANDELA

"Please, when you tell this story, say nice things about Corporal Candela. I never got the chance to thank her for believing me. She cried when we said goodbye. She couldn't believe I was being arrested," Belén requests.

When Belén finally comes to from the anesthesia, she is surrounded by police officers. One of the men in uniform looks at her vagina. They ask where the fetus is. She is still adjusting to the news that she'd been pregnant and not known it, as well as to the news that she had miscarried, so she says nothing. Then a male nurse walks up to her with a small cardboard box. Inside is something small and black. He shows it to her and says: "This is your son. Look what you did, bitch."

Belén cries and shouts that she didn't do anything, she doesn't know what they're talking about. They give her water to calm her down. It is day now and she is kept in the hospital under police custody. When she looks at the officer, she wishes she were dead. He is her best friend's boyfriend, Raúl.

"What's going on? This is a mistake, it's got to be. I was sent here on a homicide. There has to be a mix-up."

"Raúl, I'm so lucky they sent you. Tell them I'm innocent. We saw each other last week, remember? Tell them we saw each other last week and I wasn't pregnant. Come on, you know I would tell my oldest friend if I was pregnant."

He tries to calm her down, saying he's sure they've made some mistake. He leaves her alone in the room. Belén breathes a sigh of relief. Little does she know that she is getting ahead of herself.

Raúl is told there is no mistake, Belén is definitely being detained in the hospital for homicide. "But I know her," he tries to explain, "and she wasn't pregnant."

"Don't say that again, unless you want trouble. A public prosecutor already took the case, and he says she was pregnant."

Raúl doesn't know what to do. He realizes there isn't much he *can* do. All he asks is to be relieved from duty for the day. He doesn't want to go back in there and tell Belén his hands are tied.

His request is granted. He will not see Belén again.

The prosecutor assigned to her case is Washington Dávila. He's the one who decides Belén should remain "in custody" in the hospital. She sees a woman walk in. It's Corporal Candela. Belén asks after Raúl, but the officer has no idea what happened. This is when Belén begins to lose hope.

She is in pain, dizzy. She asks her mom for help. She's scared of what her dad will think when he finds out.

The following day she tries her best to get some sleep. She asks for a sleeping pill and prays it's all a nightmare. When she wakes up, a priest is staring at her with a frighteningly serious expression and a Bible in his hand. "What you've done is incredibly serious. God's law cannot be broken. You murdered your son. God will punish you. You must repent," she recalls him saying. Belén tells him she didn't do it, she's innocent. For days, weeks, months, she will say the same thing.

Candela asks the priest to vacate the room; the patient is under medical orders to rest. It's a lie. The hospital no longer cares what happens to Belén. They just want her to leave as soon as possible. The priest continues his rounds.

Candela asks Belén why she is being held there and Belén tells her everything. "No, that isn't right at all. They can't possibly detain you for that," she rages.

Corporal Candela was the first person to believe Belén. Maybe it was a matter of female empathy, or perhaps class solidarity. In Tucumán, as in many provinces with devastated industrial sectors and no retraining or reskilling initiatives, being a police or corrections officer is one of the easiest professional routes for the lower middle class. Three of Belén's cousins are police officers and two work in the prison system.

"I'm going to help you. I don't know how, but I will. As a rule, people never believe us women. But don't worry, I believe you. Even if you go to prison, never forget you're innocent. Sometimes, prison can make you forget that. But don't you ever forget it," Corporal Candela tells her.

Belén spends four days and four nights in custody at the hospital, first with Raúl and then with Candela. Once she is finally strong enough to stand, she gets discharged.

When the patrol car comes to get Belén, Candela throws her arms around her and bursts into tears. She puts her job on the line when she tells the officers about to handcuff Belén not to do it, please, they can't take her away, it isn't fair. One officer cries while the two others handcuff Belén. As they lead her through the corridors to the hospital entrance, Belén wonders what people must be thinking of her. That she's a criminal? A murderer? The officers take her to the patrol car.

In the morning, the men's prison casts the hospital in shadow. This is the last thing Belén sees when she leaves the hospital to the Special Investigations Unit of the Tucumán Police Department. Five days later she is transferred to the women's correctional facility.

12

IN THE EMERGENCY ROOM

I travel to Tucumán to retrace Belén's movements. I want to visit Avellaneda Hospital in the very early morning, the same time Belén and her mother were there.

When the taxi stops, I start shaking. Opposite the medical center loom the prison walls. They are a mirror image of the hospital.

An obese woman in shabby clothes stands on the sidewalk selling food out of a cart that lets out thick, rancid fumes. It's the only food cart in sight. They sell bollos and tortillas de rescoldo, bread rolls and flatbreads made of flour, fat, baking powder, and yeast. The woman has customers—it's late at night, and anyone who is hungry either has to eat what they have with them or resort to the offerings of that old heap that reeks of oil.

A man and several children stand barefoot on the sidewalk. Two women are breastfeeding, both startlingly thin.

I steel myself and go inside. I glance around for a seat, look at the patient check-in line, and feel faint. Until I realize it's the pediatric emergency room. There aren't any serious cases here, only that widespread vulnerability that seems to have no cure. I approach the man at the admission desk and ask him where I can find the adult emergency room. He tells me to go back outside, turn left, and reenter the building.

The first difference I notice between the pediatric ER and the adult one is that anyone entering the adult ER has to walk down a corridor in which two police officers are posted. At first I thought they were in uniform because an injured patient was being held in custody. But no, at Avellaneda Hospital, police officers perform clerical tasks. They work at the admission desk and call out patients' names when it's their turn to be seen.

I already know what to say if someone asks what I'm doing: I'm waiting for a friend. But no one asks me anything, though a few people do give me curious looks, much as we all do in emergency rooms. Inside, I am thinking about how my dad was from Tucumán and his whole family lives here. I feel like one of them, though I don't know if anyone else sees me that way. I know I'm not one of them. I have a comfortable home to go back to, people to call. They might not. If I had gone to the hospital that night, I would have had someone to ask for help, or someone to complain to about how I was treated.

I ask one of the officers where the bathroom is. I want to use the same one Belén went to that night. But the officer tells me I have to use the one near the entrance, the handicap bathroom. I lock the door. The smell of urine is so intense I can hardly breathe. I can't bring myself to sit down. The door handle is damp. The first thing I do is wash my hands. I look into the bottom of the toilet bowl, which is right there—it isn't very deep. I can't take my eyes off it. The hole is small, and the toilet walls high. Could Belén have been here?

A feeling stronger than empathy takes shape inside me. It drags me across time, shakes me. I'd also pushed out a fetus in a bathroom.

I rush out, leery the officers will have noticed I didn't flush, meaning that I didn't do anything in there. There are more police uniforms in here than scrubs and white coats. They follow me in silence. I wonder why it's necessary.

I sit down. The two girls in the seats next to me are watching videos on a cell phone and laughing nonstop.

There is the distant sound of a baby crying. It's coming from the maternity ward and the pediatric emergency room. The crying mixes with the laughter.

I gaze at a girl with long, dark hair and pink shoes sitting next to her mother in the row opposite me. She looks feverish and in pain. And sad, too, perhaps from the pain. Her mom is trying to distract her. The girl is probably the same age as Belén had been that night. What if she hemorrhages and gets escorted out of the hospital in handcuffs?

The hospital corridors don't look too bad. I'd heard everything was falling to pieces. Now there is a single broken chair. I wander down the corridors. On the surface, everything looks fine. But I wonder about the spaces where emergency patients are taken to be examined. There is a small room across the patio with the sign HEMOTHERAPY, but it's closed and in darkness. How do people with medical emergencies get seen? And by whom?

There are no nurses in sight. A doctor cuts across the corridor. All around are police officers busying themselves with the hospital's clerical tasks.

I think I've seen enough. I feel like an imposter sitting here. I go outside. Everything I'd witnessed earlier is still there, as if fixed on a canvas. Bare feet, fumes, emaciation, the silence emanating from the prison, the racket, and the scent of grilled dough. I get back in the taxi and Víctor, my driver, asks me how it went. I tell him I don't understand what kind of person would put a hospital next to a prison. I've said this to him several times already.

The first thing I do back at the hotel is wash my hands in the bathroom. I also pee in a decent-smelling toilet. There are no cops around. I want to write to Soledad Deza. Or to the journalist María

Moreno, who encourages me and edits my work. I want to tell them how I'm feeling. I also get the urge to phone Belén, and picture her sleeping peacefully eight hundred miles from there.

But it's four in the morning.

On my laptop I write, "Belén was always innocent." Then I can sleep. Tomorrow the sun will rise again over Tucumán.

13

LOCKED UP

It's Belén's first day at the Special Investigations Unit, and she would rather not talk to anyone. But another detainee approaches her and asks what she's in for. Belén says she's been charged with inducing an abortion. The woman bursts out laughing and says that can't be right. "If it was, then I'd be facing life. I've had three," she reassures her. Belén wants to explain that she didn't induce anything, but the woman insists that even if that were the case, no one gets sent to prison for an abortion.

Belén tells herself it's probably all just a big mix-up, that surely they'll release her soon. But five days pass and instead of releasing her, they take her first statement. Prosecutor Washington Dávila charges her with "homicide aggravated by relationship." Belén once again denies any wrongdoing and recounts her stay in the hospital.

They take her to Penitentiary Unit Number 4, the only women's correctional facility in Tucumán. It's in Banda del Río Salí, a neighborhood on the outskirts of Gran San Miguel de Tucumán, about twenty minutes from the center of the city. Google this town and you will find news reports that mention "shootings," "a midnight assault," and "neighbors report feeling unsafe."

The first time I visit the correctional center I ask the cab driver if Banda del Río Salí is as dangerous as people say, and he tells me it isn't. "But it's my neighborhood. I've never had any trouble," he explains.

Belén is taken to the prison in a patrol car belonging to the Tucumán Police Department. She is met by the prison warden, who talks her through the rules. "Behave, and we'll get along just fine." She tells her the schedule for breakfast, lunch, dinner, and outdoor time. A very young prison guard walks her to where she will be sleeping, in one of the cells. It's a bunk bed, with a little area off to the side for her to store her things. The other inmates look at her. There are about forty women total, ten per cell. Some say hello. Belén doesn't speak.

There is no legal reasoning for why Belén is incarcerated immediately after receiving pretrial detention. At least two conditions have to be met to justify preventive detention. One is flight risk, although it's impossible to imagine someone in Belén's condition plotting an escape. The other is the belief that the accused would pose a risk to the victims if he or she were to be released. In this case, the only victim is Belén.

A week prior, Belén had been planning her weekend with her boyfriend. Now she is alone and surrounded by stares—some sympathetic, many sad, others curious, some lost, others opaque. No one judges her. In prison, people don't talk about why they are there.

Her mom brings her some clothes, a toothbrush, and toothpaste. As she is handing these things over, the two are informed that from then on they will have to respect visiting hours, which are on Wednesdays and Sundays.

It's odd, but after a while Belén starts to feel safer in prison than she did at the Special Investigations Unit. Then again, there's the shame. She doesn't want anyone asking her why she is there. She has no interest in talking about what happened. All she wants is to go home and wake up from this nightmare.

At the facility are also Susana and Nélida, two former nuns sentenced to prison by the Supreme Court of Tucumán for murdering a teacher who went missing in 2006, her body never to be found. The case shook Tucumán. The two ex-novices, who would eventually get married, had been on bad terms with Betty, a teacher at the religious school where she'd recently been promoted to principal. Betty never assumed the new position, which Susana also had her sights set on, because one morning, shortly after leaving her house, she was murdered.

Then there is Daniela Milhein, one of the women sentenced for a case known as Marita Verón, in reference to the young woman whose disappearance led the police to uncover the sex-trafficking ring responsible for kidnapping, sexually exploiting, and holding hostage young women from the northwestern region of Argentina. Daniela is accused of holding Marita Verón hostage before she was moved to La Rioja, the last place she was seen alive.

But the majority are being held for misdemeanors, and a few others for drug trafficking.

It is all too common for drug traffickers to recruit vulnerable women who are desperate for quick cash, be it due to family debt, the need to pay for their children's medical treatments, or simply to buy food. These so-called mules are perfect candidates for this class of illegal activity: they take on huge risks for very little money and never turn on anyone when they're arrested, because they have no information about the business. The drug-trafficking ring doesn't care about them, which is how they wind up stuck right where they are: in prison.

A few women approach Belén to welcome her. She feels comfortable with some, but not so with others. The two married ex-nuns eye her with hostility from the get-go.

At night, one of the nuns, who is transitioning from female to male, visits Belén when she is trying to fall asleep. "Hey, baby. You're a pretty one. Why don't you come with us?" she suggests. Belén jumps out of bed and says: "No." The woman, who is large, insists impatiently. "All the women who come here go through us. You'd better, too, if you don't want trouble," she warns her. Belén surprises everyone by shouting: "I'd sooner be dead than with you. Leave me alone. You'd better not come near me ever again!" She screams so loudly that she wakes the prison guards and gets the attention of a few of the other inmates in her cellblock who have relative power. "Leave her alone. That's enough," they say, getting between Belén and the larger woman.

Now Belén knows who not to join up with in prison. Also, that even though some women are willing to help her, she will have to stick up for herself. She's going to have to be strong so they don't break her.

After that episode, Belén gets another invitation to leave her cellblock. This time for the room of Silvia and Vanessa, both sentenced to life in prison for murder, and Gastón, a trans man who is being held in the women's correctional facility. Silvia got life for murdering her husband after years of physical and psychological abuse. No one discusses the reason for Vanessa's sentence. Being around Gastón and the two women puts Belén at ease. The prison guards eye her with a mix of sorrow and tenderness. She seems young to them, practically a little girl, somewhat fragile. So long as no one provokes her.

GET ME OUT OF HERE

Belén asks her mother to do everything she can to get her out of prison. Her head is still spinning. She finds out her boyfriend is angry, so she sends word to him that she never wants to see his face again. The man who was recently her boyfriend is now a stranger.

The women's correctional facility in Tucumán is relatively tranquil in comparison with the men's. While their permanent population tends to fluctuate between thirty-five to fifty inmates at a time, the largest men's prison in San Miguel de Tucumán holds an average of one thousand inmates. Next to the massive carceral structure in Villa Urquiza, the women's facility resembles a small school in a poor neighborhood superintended by an armed principal and a group of prison guards who would easily work anywhere else if they could.

But the women and trans people there are deprived of freedom; they are punished and kept behind bars. They are living through their own personal hell. And Belén has a childlike innocence.

Belén's mother, Beatriz, makes an appointment with a lawyer someone recommended to her. His name is Abraham Musi. Beatriz doesn't know this, but Musi is a former criminal prosecutor who was fired for his involvement in a case of so-called twin cars, in which forged registrations and license plates were assigned to stolen vehicles. All she knows is that he's a criminal lawyer who can get her daughter out of prison.

The lawyer asks for a retainer. It's a long, difficult month—March, the start of the school year—but Beatriz scrapes together the money with help from Belén's father, siblings, and aunts. She and one of Belén's sisters apply for a loan because they're the only ones with proof of income. Anything to get her daughter out.

Musi visits Belén in prison and informs her that a DNA test was conducted on the dead fetus. Based on the results, he says, she is definitely getting life in prison. Belén insists they made the whole thing up. She tries to get the lawyer to believe her, but he says the evidence tells a different story. That he can't get her out of prison.

Weeks pass without news from Musi. Beatriz calls him repeatedly but can't get him to take a meeting with her. She is distressed and impatient at the lack of response. Visiting hours are that weekend, but she doesn't want to see Belén unless she has some hope to give her. So she shows up in person at Musi's office on Friday afternoon, when she thinks he'll have returned from his siesta. The lawyer grudgingly agrees to meet with her. He asks for double what he was paid to continue working with Belén. "It's a challenging case. What she did warrants life in prison," he insists.

Beatriz is demoralized. Raising the money for the retainer had been incredibly difficult. There's no way she can get him the amount he's asking for now.

The family finally manages to round up more money for Musi. But it isn't enough, and he drops the case. This is how, from one day to the next, Belén finds herself without a lawyer.

Although Musi may not be handling Belén's case anymore, he is himself under investigation for forging personal and vehicular documents. In June 2018 the federal district court finds former prosecutor Héctor Alfredo Abraham Musi guilty of abusing power, violating the oath of office, and committing irregularities in the creation of public instruments. He is sentenced to three years in prison and disqualified from holding public office for four years. In the end, he receives time served. He spends not one day in prison.

It was only five years after Belén's initial arrest, in June 2019, that Belén's sister was able to pay off the loan she took out so that Musi would get Belén released from prison, something he never made any effort to do.

15

SHE CRIES

Meanwhile, time passes in prison. Belén thinks about her dad a lot. It makes her sad not to see him. But she wants him to see her as a free woman. He too wants to see her as a free woman. *Maybe he believes I'm guilty? I want to explain everything to him, but I can't do it while I'm locked up in here*, she muses.

Sometimes she closes her eyes and thinks back to her high school boyfriend, Jorge. It's possible she'll never see him again. It's possible he won't believe her either when he finds out.

The World Cup is on, and everyone's minds are on Messi, Lavezzi, and Mascherano. Outside people dream of Argentina making it to the final. Meanwhile, she dreams of freedom. The inmates cry during the penalty shootout against the Netherlands on July 9, 2014. They feel closer to São Paulo than to the Casa Histórica de Tucumán. Mascherano tells goalkeeper Sergio Romero: Today is your chance to become a hero. Belén goes to bed and, when no one is around, she cries.

She cries when her visitors leave. She cries when someone is short with her.

She cries when she remembers she is locked up.

She cries because she doesn't know what will become of her. She cries because she doesn't know what her father thinks of her.

She cries when thinking about the past, all the facts that led her into this situation, how her ex-boyfriend let her down, abandoned her, blamed her for what happened.

She cries because she never realized she was expecting the baby she so suddenly lost.

She cries because instead of hugging her, they sent her to prison.

She cries because no one puts her mind at ease, telling her everything will be all right.

She cries because they don't believe her. She cries.

16

A CHRISTMAS PRESENT

Belén is offered a job in the kitchen. She accepts. She has to do *something* until she's released. She clocks in at ten a.m. and out at eight p.m. She loves to cook and eat. Given all the hours there are in a day, it isn't long before she's perfected all kinds of prison meals. She'd always wanted to do the seals on empanadas just like her mom. Only in the prison kitchen does she figure out how.

Mondays are for empanadas, Wednesdays for milanesa sandwiches, and Fridays for pizza.

Saturdays are the best day because the home economics teacher leads a cooking workshop at the prison, an excuse to make them mouthwatering stews. Apparently, her stews are the only thing the women miss when they leave prison.

Belén receives a modest salary for working in the kitchen. She gives most of it to her mom when she visits, to help pay back the loan she and her sister took out for the lawyer. Ever since Belén did a workshop on handicrafts and party favors, she's used whatever's left of her salary to buy fabric.

She's finally found a pastime she likes: making costumes. She gets a few commissions from inmates who have children outside prison. They ask her for princess and superhero costumes. For herself, she makes a Snow White costume and another of the clown Piñón Fijo.

"Why would you dress up as that clown?" the other inmates ask her. *Why not?* She doesn't want to explain herself, but the idea of dressing up as Piñón Fijo and surprising her niece for Christmas fills her with excitement.

December is around the corner, and by now it's clear Belén won't be getting out in time for the holidays. She'll have to think of another surprise for her niece Delfina. She learns to make stuffed plush toys and decides to sew her niece a large dog with a big smile that she can cuddle in bed at night—at least until Belén gets out and she and Delfina can cuddle instead. Belén doesn't speak to anyone. Instead, she pours all her energy into the stuffed dog. She throws away several attempts because she wants it to be perfect.

It's December 24, and Belén eagerly awaits her mother. She's so excited to give her the plush toy. Suddenly, she realizes she'd like to get a Christmas present, too. The year before, Belén had dressed up as Santa Claus, they'd eaten a suckling pig her brother had brought over from Salta, and her sister had given her a necklace.

She spends all morning waiting. She asks to speak to the prison warden so she can stare out the window and see her mother when she walks in. But Beatriz doesn't show up until the afternoon.

"Sorry, I almost didn't make it. Your cousins in Simoca are coming as well, so there's going to be a lot of us," she tells her. What she doesn't say is that without Belén, whose salary used to help pay for the shopping, and with the loan payments, they can barely afford Christmas dinner. No one is getting presents this year.

Belén shows her the stuffed dog she made for Delfina. It's huge and brown, with big floppy ears. "I didn't have time to make you anything," she says.

"There's no room in the house for stuffed animals. The only thing I'm praying for tonight is your release, honey," her mother promises.

They clasp each other's hands and hug. Belén tells her she should leave—she's got a lot of cooking to do. But the truth is, she doesn't want her mother to see her crying.

At midnight the inmates raise glasses of nonalcoholic cider. A few women open the presents their families and loved ones dropped off for them. All in all, they've made a lot more gifts than they've received.

There was no Christmas miracle. Belén went to sleep far away from her family. There wasn't a single gift for her under the small penitentiary Christmas tree made of wreaths. She never felt as sad as she did that night.

17

OPEN THE DOORS (TO GO OUT AND PLAY)

After just under a year in prison, Belén decides to leave the kitchen to work in the garden. Being locked up has started weighing more and more on her. At least she gets some sunshine outdoors. There's always something to do in the garden, such as watering plants and painting walls. But she doesn't leave the kitchen fully behind, either. She's drawn there by the sweets and milanesa sandwiches they eat once a month. And by kitchen manager Victoria, who still works there. She wants to introduce Belén to her grandson. "He's sweet and has a good heart. Just like you," is how she describes him.

She always goes out to the yard at the sound of a Ulises Bueno song. She swears to herself she will dance to it when she gets out.

Nélida still harasses her now and then. She never forgave Belén for rejecting her and makes fun of her every chance she gets. She gives her the nickname *La Llorona*, or "crybaby." It's true Belén cries a lot in prison, especially after her niece visits. But she does it in secret. She adores the girl and doesn't like being apart from her. She doesn't like her niece seeing her in prison; she wants to go outside and play with her.

Reading is the one thing that stops Belén from crying and discourages people from bothering her. A librarian drops in once a week with a small key to a three-by-three-foot bookcase in the main common area. There are no more than thirty books. The librarian is responsible for opening and closing the bookcase and jotting down the titles of the books that the inmates check out. He'd often been afraid of losing that job. But ever since Belén's arrival, he knows at least one inmate will ask him for a book. Belén always checks one out, sometimes even the same novel. She's read *Kiss of the Spider Woman* three times. The conversations Valentín and Molina have in Manuel Puig's novels make her forget she's in prison.

It's 2015, and people are getting ready to vote in the general elections. The Belén case is at a standstill. The only thing that matters during campaign cycles is the election, and incarcerated people are promptly forgotten. The women watch the Susana Giménez talk show and learn that a demonstration will be held on June 3 to protest all the women who have died. The most important women's march in Argentina is being organized. Some of the inmates work with the prison guards to make a sign that says #NiUnaMenos ("Not One Less"). But they will be the only ones who see it.

The relationship between prison guards and inmates is often one of camaraderie, sometimes even friendship. They share an obligation to obey and very little hope for a better future. But with Belén, things go a bit further: the guards look out for her. One night Belén is reading *Open the Door (to Go Out and Play)*, a book of poems by Ana Guillot. The two prison guards on shift chuckle and ask if she'd like to go outside.

"We have to take the trash out. Are you up for it?"

To do so, she would have to leave the prison. The guards have discussed among themselves and come to the conclusion that Belén doesn't deserve to be in prison. "We'll think of an excuse if she runs. Though she'd have to leave," they say to convince themselves.

Belén carries the trash bag through a grilled door. Then another. She looks out at the street, a single gate standing between them. She feels dizzy and walks up to the last guard. She's sure the guard won't let her pass. But he opens the gate. She's being let out.

Belén is on the sidewalk outside the correctional facility. She is unhandcuffed and unsupervised. The prison guards watch her from inside the prison and wonder if they will ever see her again. They can always make something up, they're not worried.

But Belén leaves the trash bags on the corner and walks back. She asks the guard to open the gate, then asks to be let back into the prison. She walks through a grilled door, then another. She is inside again.

The guards laugh. "You weren't up to it. You looked like a cat that can't be bothered to go outside."

"I'll go out when they prove my innocence. You'll see," Belén replies.

She goes back to her book.

> *How long can people live without air?*
> *How long?*
> *What is the measure of suffocation?*

And falls asleep.

On December 10 a new president is elected in Argentina, Mauricio Macri, and a new governor in Tucumán, Juan Luis Manzur. For Belén, nothing has changed.

> *May every person play their game*
> *May the rose be a rose*
> *Smooth and plane sheer with sun.*

TUCUMÁN IS THE NEW BLACK

The streets of San Miguel de Tucumán are lined with orange trees. No one picks the oranges because they're bitter and inedible, although they do make for a nice view. People hurled them at the governor's house in the protests following reports of electoral fraud in the 2015 election.

Belén doesn't remember hearing about this protest. No one in prison heard about the hurled oranges.

I travel to Tucumán. I want to see the prison where Belén was held. I arrange this with Estela, who teaches workshops at the facility.

If not for the sign on the door that says the building is a correctional center, you might think it was a school or a hospital in a poor neighborhood, save for the dogs wandering around inside. There are no high walls, and the bars visible from the outside are those of the main gate. There are disassembled kids' toys.

It's raining heavily when we get there, and the main gate is muddy. Loud shouts are coming from inside, though it's hard to understand what's being said. Estela knocks, and a police officer ushers us in. Two dogs slip in behind us and seek shelter at the entrance.

Everyone there knows Estela and greets her. The first thing anyone sees when they walk in is a huge image of Christ gazing down at them with the words I TRUST YOU. Estela asks about the shouts we just heard, and they tell her it's the evangelicals who organize hymn sessions when they visit the prison. "They've gone over again. They keep staying longer and longer. I'm going to tell them their time's up," says the woman running the facility that Saturday.

Most of the prison guards are young, shy-looking women. One of them shows me her lace-up boots and says they get very hot, that sometimes her feet burn up in the summer.

The evangelical ceremony ends. The only thing I managed to make out were the words "Praise the Lord," over and over. They leave, but not before giving every one of the inmates a Bible. One woman doesn't go up for one, because she's busy making stuffed toys at a table, cutting colorful fabric. I imagine this is what Belén must have done, too.

In the main common area, where workshops are held, visitors welcomed, and evangelicals sing hymns, the same image of Christ that hangs in the entrance hall is everywhere, in varying sizes. There are multiple Christs plastered on each wall. "I trust you," Jesus says again. There is also an image of the Virgin Mary.

Estela asks the inmates to sit down so she can discuss their health with them one-on-one. She asks if they're getting regular medical checkups. The majority say yes, yet nearly all of them have the same problem: they can't see.

Of the twenty-five women sitting in the room, close to twenty of them can't see clearly enough to read. Some are shortsighted, while others have cataracts, a few diabetes, and a handful are farsighted. The eye doctor hasn't been to the prison in years.

The previous one moved away, and they haven't found a replacement. There's no time frame for their vision to improve, because there's no one around to deal with it.

Maybe that's why the librarian stopped coming and now the bookcase is always locked.

The home economics teacher who used to make them stew and teach them to cook is also gone. There are no ingredients for the recipes. They aren't served beef anymore, only chicken every once in a while. "We fill up on bread because there isn't a lot of food. And loads of polenta. The diabetic women get special meals, but the meals only last two days. Then they have to eat bread like the rest of us."

She says the quantity and quality of the food is decreasing. One of the women complains about the cats. She says they eat breakfast, dinner, and sleep with the cats all over them. At the moment, there are fifty cats and thirty-five inmates. Besides the smell, the cats have also made holes in the roof from sharpening their claws. I remember a news report that went viral a few days ago featuring photographs of a rat infestation at a men's prison in Tucumán. I'd sooner have cats than rats, I think—until I smell them and see one eat food right off a girl's plate. Even so, I'm pretty sure I'd rather have cats. Except I'm not the one behind bars and hopefully will never have to choose which of them to share a meal with.

One of the inmates asks where I'm from. When I say Buenos Aires, she tells me she's going to move there as soon as she gets out; she has a job lined up in the Once neighborhood. When I ask Estela about it, she says she doubts the woman will be getting out anytime soon. After completing her sentence, she was caught stealing again.

I don't ask about the other inmates. I recognize one of the former nuns because there's a petition for surgery in his medical-request form. He started transitioning in prison. As a matter of course, all trans people are sent to women's correctional facilities. The chances of them surviving at a men's prison are slim. "Please, Estela. Don't forget about me. I want to be a man when I die," he pleads when we pass him.

I keep walking around the prison and talking to women who are there for reasons unknown to me. I realize some are doing time for murder and others for stealing, and that many are inside because they covered for a partner or family member. I'm sure there are other wrongful convictions like Belén's.

We exit the building into a small yard. In one corner, a group of women is listening to cumbia. In another, they're listening to cuartetazo.

Two of the inmates are dancing.

"Come dance," they beckon.

A woman sits on the ground smoking cigarettes, eyes welling with tears. She tells us she is trying to survive. I wish I knew what she needed. Then again, maybe it's selfish of me to want to know, given that I probably can't help her.

One woman is throwing random objects at the cats with an expression of uncontrollable glee. Besides eye issues, they also have skin problems. They reckon it has something to do with the fact that many of the cats have scabies.

"Come smell them. Some of the cats are rotten through with scabies," says an inmate whose face is covered in abrasions.

One woman is reading *El jardín de las delicias* by Marco Denevi, a rewriting of Greek myths with a humorous, erotic twist.

Another tells us: "I can't sleep." She's shaking. "The psychiatrist promised to get me meds, but they aren't helping. I want to be put to sleep. I can't take it anymore. I'm losing my mind." She talks and shakes. She looks like she's having an acute anxiety attack. Although I want to give her some Rivotril, I know I'm not allowed. One woman asks for locro, a hominy stew that is Argentina's national dish, even though she's ill and knows it's not the best thing for her to be eating.

There is a woman so big and strong she was given the nickname King Kona. She's in prison for beating an employee of a love hotel to death. Barring King Kona, Belén spent time in prison with most of the women who are still here today. Before we leave, Estela asks the prison warden to call the psychiatrist so she can do something for the woman with anxiety.

"She's coming in five days. We'll give her a placebo in the meantime. Maybe it'll help," she says half-heartedly.

19

THE PATH TO TRIAL

Belén's family spent every last penny they had and all the money they borrowed on the lawyer who dropped her case. They can't afford to hire another. In court, Belén is informed that if she doesn't get a lawyer, the state will appoint her a public defender.

In Argentina the right to counsel enshrines the figure of the federal public defender. Public servants of the federal government go through a rigorous selection process and are in high demand—not only by those who don't have the resources to retain a private attorney but also by those who want to ensure they get the best possible defense. The public servants of Tucumán Province, on the other hand, are neither subject to the same requirements, nor as high profile as their federal counterparts. And they aren't sought out by people who can afford private representation. Their services are reserved for the truly poor, so they tend to receive little social or legal oversight.

When Belén hears she's being appointed a public defender, she feels hopeful. Her family won't have to spend any more money on a lawyer. On top of that, her lawyer is a woman. If the corporal at the hospital believed her, how could her own defense attorney not?

But days pass, and weeks, then months with no word from her

counsel. Every waiting moment brings her closer and closer to her former unease.

Belén doesn't know this, but Prosecutor Washington Dávila is stoking the idea that she committed murder and gathering statements to that effect.

HIGH HEELS

As her trial draws near, Belén finds out she will finally get to meet her lawyer.

The first thing she sees and hears are her high heels. She should have let that click-clack drown out the words that came out of the woman's mouth. "I'm your attorney. Your pregnancy was very late stage—thirty-two weeks—so you're going to have to take responsibility," she fires out without bothering to ask any questions. Belén replies:

"What do you mean? What are you talking about? I was never eight months pregnant."

"Honey, I know. Listen to me. You're better off admitting to what you've done."

"But that never happened. How are you going to defend me if you don't believe me?"

In response, silence. Only the face of someone who refuses to listen or consider anything she says. Belén feels crushed, guilty even, because that's how she's being told to feel. And yet the injustice sours her shame into anger; she wants to shout so someone will listen. At the same time, it feels pointless. With the exception of her mom and her sister, it's like no one is willing to listen.

Belén's trial is around the corner, and she feels unmoored. She doesn't want any visitors. She fulfills her prison duties but stays quiet, talking to no one. Her last hope just went out the window.

THE MEETING

Three years ago, Soledad Deza was sitting at work in the same office where we would meet for the first time, talking to the youngest member of her team, the lawyer Luciana Gramaglio, whom she mostly refers to as Luli.

The phone rings, and a woman asks to speak to her. She says she's part of a team of psychologists working on the case of a woman accused of homicide and inducing an abortion. She knows Soledad specializes in abortion issues and wonders if she can give her some counsel. Her question is about the limitations of professional confidentiality. Soledad tells her how it works, and then they hang up.

A couple of hours later, the phone rings again. It's the same woman. "Mrs. Deza, I don't know if I mentioned this, but the case I called about is from two years ago," she says.

"No, you didn't," Soledad replies.

"Mrs. Deza, a young woman is in prison," the woman says in a low, afflicted voice. They hang up.

"What was all that about, Sole?" Luli asks.

"A woman in Tucumán is in prison for an abortion," Soledad replies, although she's having a hard time believing it. She never saw the case on the news, and no one ever mentioned it to her. If a woman was in prison for an abortion, every women's organization in the area would have known about it. It's the twenty-first century. How can a woman in Argentina be thrown in prison for an abortion without causing an uproar? But deep down, she knows that the woman she just spoke to on the phone called her office to make sure she found out. To make sure she knew.

Soledad practically runs to the courthouse, where she verifies the existence of the case. She's already made up her mind to do something about it. At court she learns that the medical team is testifying the next day. Closing arguments and the verdict are scheduled for five days later, on the following Monday.

Later that day, in the dead of night, Soledad takes out her laptop and writes an email to the women of the National Campaign for Abortion, which she's been involved with for the past couple of years.

To: Campaign
Subject: Prison for abortion in Tucumán

Compañeras, yesterday someone called my office to tell me that a woman in the area was sent to prison 2 years ago for an abortion. Her doctors reported her to the police.
 I'm meeting her at the prison tomorrow at 9 a.m. Her trial started today.
 I hope I can do something for her!
 I'll keep you posted.

Soledad

By eight a.m. the following morning, a Saturday, Soledad is already in her car on her way to the women's correctional facility. She is met by the prison guards' supervisor. "I need to speak with Belén," she says. The woman tells her that won't be possible. Belén has to approve every visitor. Soledad pulls out her card and asks them to let Belén know she's there to help. But there's nothing she can do, so she goes back home.

She can't concentrate on anything during lunch. Her husband and children ask if she's OK. She says she is fine, but the truth is she feels restless. She has the sense her life is about to change.

She goes out to the garden during siesta to smoke and think. Until a phone call interrupts her. It's Belén's mother. Belén must have given her Soledad's number. She's agitated. She just heard Belén could get life and begs Soledad to visit her in prison the next day.

Sunday, April 17, dawns cold and rainy. Soledad arrives at the prison. They're expecting her. In the screening process, during which visitors are inspected for objects that could be of use to detainees, whether for pleasure or potential danger, they make her leave her wallet.

They usher her into a small, makeshift visiting room. After a while, she hears Belén's voice for the first time.

"Who wants to see me?" Belén asks.

Belén glimpses the silhouette of a short, thin woman drenched in rain and holding a cigarette.

"It's me, honey," Soledad replies.

They are now face-to-face. They hug. Instead of speaking, Belén cries. Soledad starts crying as well. For a few minutes, only their hands touch. They grip each other, damp from the tears that mix with the raindrops Soledad brought in. The drops of water Belén sheds are not from the outside. They're tears of captivity and despair.

Soledad introduces herself. She says she's a lawyer and a member of the National Campaign for Abortion. That she's there to help her. She gives her a book called *Jaque a la reina*, then says:

"I want you to know you shouldn't be in here. You should be free. I brought you a book I wrote about a young woman called María Magdalena, who's a bit like you. The doctors who treated her at the hospital accused her of having an abortion. And that's not right. Medical staff have a duty of care. It's the same in your case. María Magdalena is free. You should be free, too."

Belén tells Soledad she's been in prison for more than two years and that the doctors said awful things about her last Thursday at the "trial." They accused her of doing things she hadn't done. "How can they believe I would do something like that?" she asks Soledad. She starts crying again. Soledad cries, too, and asks what evidence they're using to charge her.

Belén looks at her with surprise and says she doesn't know, they never told her. And she hasn't read her case.

Three hours fly by. Belén asks Soledad to represent her. But closing arguments are scheduled for the next day, and Soledad doesn't have enough time to read the docket.

"I'm coming to court with you tomorrow. Try to relax. I'm here to get you out, sweetie," she promises.

They hug goodbye.

Soledad gets back in her car and drives home through unceasing rain.

Belén reads the María Magdalena book. She asks the warden for a pencil so she can underline the parts that speak to her.

To: Campaign
Subject: Re: Prison for abortion in Tucumán

Dear compañeras:

I'm writing with an update. I just got back from the prison. Yesterday, they didn't let me in to see her (she's not giving her real name; she doesn't want anything made public yet). Yesterday, we only managed to talk on the phone. I was there today for 2 hours and left feeling incredibly sad and helpless. Here's the story:

When she arrived at Hospital Avellaneda on 03/21/2014 with her mother, she was already mid-miscarriage.

She walks into the ER and is seen by two medical residents. They give her something for the pain.

Then she goes to the bathroom and expels the fetus. She says she felt something but didn't look closely and then washed her hands. The doctor gives her a drip and tells the mother that Belén miscarried, that she was 20 weeks pregnant.

She denies knowing that she was pregnant.

She wakes up in the communal labor room surrounded by police and with forensic pathologists "checking me down there." She is held in the hospital for 5 days.

Her mother told me on the phone that in the meantime, while Belén is getting a D&C from the surgeon, a police officer goes to the same bathroom Belén had been to and finds a fetus.

She's had two lawyers. No one went to see her in the hospital.

She was held in remand for "abortion followed by homicide."

The forensic pathologists claim she was 36 weeks pregnant and that the fetus was alive at the time of birth.

They changed the caption to "first-degree murder aggravated by relationship."

I haven't seen the file, but Belén says she didn't present and that her lawyer advised her not to let her mother testify, or she would be charged as an accomplice. 3 days before the trial her lawyer resigns because the family isn't able to get together the 20,000 pesos he'd requested as an honorarium.

The Public Defender's Office takes over.

No one raised the issue of doctor-patient confidentiality, no one asked for a mistrial.

The trial started on Thursday, and the court adjourned until tomorrow when arguments will be heard.

I can't represent her tomorrow. Without access to her docket, I can't present a defense.

She's asked me to go to court with her, and I've pledged to bring a motion for a mistrial so that it's entered into the record before the court issues a ruling.

IT'S SO INCREDIBLY SAD!!!!

She doesn't want her case going public, she feels really ashamed.

I'll send an update tomorrow because there's not much I can do before then.

The bench is composed of 3 men :(Sending you hugs, compañeras!!!!!

Soledad

22

THERE WILL BE NO JUSTICE

The closing arguments are scheduled for Monday, April 18, 2016, at ten a.m. On Belén's side are her mother, her sister, two aunts, and Soledad.

The judges Dante Ibáñez, Fabián Fradejas, and Rafael Macoritto arrive on time. Prosecutor Carlos Sale walks into the courtroom. Belén enters in handcuffs and with security. She's wearing the same jacket she had on the night she went to the hospital. White and snug, with little flowers. Much as on that night, it's a mystery today whether anyone will realize Belén couldn't have worn that jacket at more than twenty-two weeks pregnant. But no one notices her.

They are focused entirely on who should be there and yet isn't. Belén's attorney, for example. In the room are the men who will judge her and the man who will accuse her, but not the woman who will defend her. It's been like this from the moment Belén set foot in the hospital. There is no one to defend her.

It's been half an hour, but they can't start without her defense counsel. The chief judge, Dante Ibáñez, expresses his annoyance and asks the clerk to fetch Norma Bulacio—as a matter of urgency. "This delay is unprofessional. We're all waiting for her." In the meantime, Belén is still handcuffed.

The defense attorney arrives a while later and apologizes. She begins her closing by presuming that Belén is guilty but claiming she was "in a state of shock," one that should have been corroborated by a medical board. She speaks of her client's "postpartum condition" at the time of the event. At no point does she deny the incident. In fact, she acknowledges it. It's as if she and Belén had never spoken.

She claims insanity.

"The psychologist and psychiatrist were faced with a woman who was insane. They interviewed her that same day. She was surrounded by doctors and police officers," she continues.

To conclude, she says: "On top of this, there is no DNA evidence."

Belén and Soledad look at one another. Neither understands what is happening. Both realize that a grave injustice is about to be committed in this courtroom. Without DNA evidence, it's impossible to affirm the existence of anything incriminating. Even the TV lawyers know this. It would seem the Supreme Court of Tucumán does not.

During the proceedings, Bulacio does not provide the court with any evidence in support of Belén's defense. Not even a picture from the days before Belén had gone to the hospital with abdominal pain. All she would've had to do to find such a picture is visit Belén's Facebook page. Belén had told her as much. Neither the public defender nor any of the men who are about to rule on Belén's case have any interest in seeing the evidence closest to hand, proof that a couple of days before Belén's hospital visit, she showed no signs of a third-trimester pregnancy.

When it's his turn to speak, the prosecutor cites the Belém do Pará Convention, an international treaty whose goal is to prevent, penalize, punish, and combat any and all violence against women. Only he doesn't cite it in defense of Belén but of her fetus.

The prosecutor requests a fourteen-year prison sentence for "first-degree homicide aggravated by relationship."

It's Belén's turn. She knows this is her only chance to finally get them to listen. She will address not only the judges but also her public defender, who has refused to listen to her until now. She will also address her family in the hopes her aunts will tell her father what she's about to say. Soledad is there to listen to her.

"First of all, I'd like to say I didn't know I was pregnant, so you can't tell me that I committed the atrocious act that I'm being accused of. How can you say I cut the umbilical cord? You can't just cut a cord. I was there when my nephew was born. They gave me an intravenous sedative and when I woke up, I was covered in blood and a police officer was looking at my private parts. Where is the DNA evidence that proves the fetus was mine? I've been kept away from my family for two years; I was kept in the hospital for five days. And you're saying I did this? I didn't hurt anyone. No one asked me how I was or if I needed any help. The psychologists approached me, and when I was taken to the delivery room no one looked after me. Then one of the staff came in and started treating me like I was a murderer. I'm being charged without evidence," she says in her defense. Then she fixes her eyes on the faces of the judges, who have already found her guilty, and questions them:

"Where is the evidence that proves that I'm the murderer you think I am?"

At that question, only one of the judges—Ibáñez—lowers his gaze. "I need to be with my family. You've kept me away from them from day one. All I'm asking for is some compassion. I'm broken. Seeing my mom leave the prison, my niece. How can you think I would ever kill someone? I've never hurt anyone, you can't accuse me of doing a thing like that. Give me a chance to be with my family. I can't take it anymore. I've had enough," she practically begs.

Soledad is perplexed. Later she will recall: "I was shocked by how ignorant the prosecutor was, how he could just overlook his violent behavior throughout the case. And what surprised me most was how much better Belén was at defending herself than either of her first two lawyers."

The truth is that the defense never once considered that their client was being tried for a crime that rested on contradictory evidence and on a timeline and witness accounts that did not match up.

The judges adjourn until the following day.

That night, Belén can't sleep. She wonders if the judges will realize the whole thing was made up, that she shouldn't be in prison.

Soledad can't sleep, either. She knows that, between the prosecutor's closing statement and a defense attorney who believes her client is guilty, it's unlikely that justice will be served.

The next day, they're all back in court: judges, prosecutor, and defense counsel. Belén arrives with the prison guards, who treat her like a sister. Two of her real sisters are also there, as are two of her aunts. Soledad has brought a friend who is a doctor.

Chief Judge Ibáñez speaks first. "This may be the most complex case we've ever had to rule on. We recognize the state's failure to combat unwanted pregnancy. We recognize the state's failure to provide adequate sexual education . . ." Before perpetrating another failure on behalf of the state, a failure of justice, he says, "But we felt obligated to consider the value of NN's life . . ." This is how Belén finds out the judges have given the fetus she never knew was in her belly a nickname.

Ever since she was accused of being a murderer more than two years ago, Belén has dreamed of the moment they tell her it was all a big mistake. She is sitting before the judges, who can't bring themselves to look at her.

"The court hereby finds the defendant guilty of murder aggravated by relationship under extraordinary mitigating circumstances and sentences her to eight years in prison."

23

SENTENCED

The judges read the verdict and exit the room. Belén and her family are left behind. She cries in the arms of her sister, who is also sobbing. After a while, they're pulled apart so Belén can be handcuffed. Soledad hugs Belén and says she will visit her in prison soon. Bulacio approaches her, but Belén doesn't let her speak. "You have no shame. One day you'll realize I'm innocent and have to apologize for not believing me," she warns.

Belén returns to prison.

"No matter what happened to me, I never lost strength. I kept telling myself: I will not fall, I will keep going, because what they're doing to me is unjust. Except for one time. There was a single time in my life when I thought I'd never recover, that I was falling and wouldn't be able to get back on my feet. It was when I left the courthouse and my mom stayed behind. I didn't think I'd get through it. It was hard, but here I am," Belén tells me three years later as we sit together at the clothing stall she works at in Constitución.

Soledad lingers in the courtroom where Belén was read her

verdict and informs Norma Bulacio that she will be taking over the case. Bulacio replies: "I wanted to tell Belén that an eight-year sentence is a win. She could have gotten life. She was let off easy. You should tell her this, too, if you're planning to take over the defense. Let me get you the brief."

What brief? Why is she happy? Soledad wonders, by then a little stunned and very exasperated.

The thing is, Bulacio is proud of having introduced the defendant's "postpartum condition" as a mitigating factor in a crime she, too, believes Belén to be guilty of. In order for a "postpartum case" to stand, there would have to be a baby, a mother, a woman who gave birth. That wasn't the case with Belén, but what does that matter now? Case closed. Who's next?

The brief Bulacio mentioned turned out to be a fifty-page file containing every piece of evidence that had led to Belén's conviction. The defense can appeal using elements of the brief to dismiss or at least call into question certain pieces of evidence. Soledad takes the documentation and says goodbye. From then on, she will be Belén's new legal counsel.

She walks into the street and peeks at the file she just received. The first thing she reads is the medical record with Belén's diagnosis, which states, "incomplete miscarriage without complications." How does a diagnosis like this one, which matches Belén's testimony, become a murder conviction?

The sense of bewilderment only grows. The timeline has been altered, dates and times don't line up. It all seems so absurd.

Soledad hails a cab. She wants to get home as fast as possible so she can keep reading. Just as she is settling into her living room armchair, her daughter gets home from school. She mixes a glass of chocolate milk for her and feels stunned all over again: the evidence rests on the testimony of physicians who are prohibited by law from disclosing any and all circumstances pertaining to their patient's health.

The prosecution's entire case rested on the violation of doctor-patient confidentiality.

The other thing that shocks Soledad is the sheer number of inconsistencies she comes across. While one medical expert had affirmed the fetus was thirty-two weeks old, the criminal investigation cited other accounts, which ranged from a fifteen-week gestation period to a pregnancy of twenty-two weeks. The fetus had aged in the file.

The summary brief Soledad is reading contains another detail no one seems to have noticed: the fetus had been found before Belén was admitted into the emergency room. In some places a female fetus is mentioned, while in others the fetus is male. It's utter nonsense.

On April 20, Soledad formally takes over Belén's defense. No one has hired her; Belén's family doesn't have money. But Soledad decides that what matters to her more than anything is for this young woman who was incarcerated for a miscarriage to go free.

She works on the defense with two other lawyers: Luciana Gramaglio and Noelia Aisama.

When Soledad goes to the courthouse to collect the docket, she realizes once again that things aren't going to be easy. She asks to photocopy the file but is told she can't. "The court is holding the docket in its offices to elaborate the grounds for the verdict."

Soledad swallows, composing herself. She explains that she recently took over this client's defense and is drafting an appeal for cassation and to end remand. She can't do this without the docket. And every passing day eats into what little time she has to file the expiring appeal. "Judge's orders," they tell her without even a glance.

Now what? Soledad asks herself. Belén was convicted of murder and found guilty without evidence. A purely legal strategy won't cut it. To clean up this mess, Soledad will have to wage a battle on two fronts: the legal and the social. The gravest injustices may be committed in secret, but executioners often buckle when brought to light.

24

HISTORY IS WRITTEN BY THE WINNERS

How do you tell the story of a woman who was deemed guilty from the very beginning, despite all evidence to the contrary? The truth isn't enough to make a story convincing. Soledad will have to be careful about how and where she chooses to tell it.

The case has to be taken to the media. *La Gaceta* is the main newspaper in Tucumán. It sets the agenda in the province and tends to be very much in lockstep with the powers that be. And that power just convicted Belén.

Now that *La Gaceta* has been ruled out, they discuss who else would take the story. With the exception of *Página 12* and the *Buenos Aires Herald*, most are wary of publishing articles on abortion.

But this time Soledad believes the story should come straight from Tucumán, told in Tucumán voices. It's a gamble but also a conviction.

This is why Soledad decides to call Celina De la Rosa, the journalist who partnered with Sebastián Pisarello—the grandson of Ángel Pisarello, a human rights lawyer who was kidnapped right in front of his family in Tucumán and later found dead, his body showing signs of torture—to found Agencia de Prensa Alternativa, or APA, an alternative news agency committed to sharing stories about social issues that big media outlets had no interest in pursuing.

"I'm in the middle of something, Sole. What's going on?"

"I need to see you. It's urgent. A woman in Tucumán has been in prison for miscarrying—"

"What?" She doesn't let her finish.

Celina finishes the interview. Twenty minutes later, she is at Soledad's house. One woman highlights the file while the other takes notes. Later, Celina takes her notes to a pizzeria, where she and Sebastián discuss how they can best present the case to the world.

The decision to share news about the case has been made. But they don't want to do anything without consulting Belén.

25

I'M BELÉN

Soledad visits Belén in prison to ask her input on their strategy. Belén doesn't want the media talking about her incarceration; she doesn't want her family to have to speak for her, for them to be pointed at in the neighborhood, or at work, or by their friends. She feels responsible for what her mom and dad, her sisters and brothers, may suffer. Her aunts and uncles, and her cousins, too. At this point she's convinced she is guilty of something. Paula, one of the prison guards who's become fond of Belén, tells her Soledad is right: what she's going through is so monumentally unjust that the only way to get the judges to reconsider is to go public.

Soledad explains that they don't have to show her face or reveal her real name to share the case. María Magdalena isn't the real name of the woman the court tried to convict for similar reasons.

The young woman we've been discussing until now goes by another name. For as long as I've been writing this book, she has asked to be referred to as Belén whenever her case is discussed.

"Pick another name for yourself," Soledad says. So much has happened in the past few days that nothing springs to mind. She likes the names of her sisters and cousin but doesn't think it would be a good idea to use one of those.

"You could call yourself Belén, if you want," Soledad says. She laughs with surprise. "You don't like it? What about María Belén?" Soledad asks enthusiastically.

"No, I like it. Just Belén," she says.

"Perfect." Soledad smiles. "So, I'm your lawyer, Soledad Deza. Who are you?"

"I'm Belén," she says, also laughing.

26

FROM TUCUMÁN
TO THE WORLD

Soledad and Celina meet again. They work together to draft the first press release about Belén's case. The story, which until now has been written by the health care and legal systems and governed by the idea that all women who fail to give birth are guilty, is now being rewritten by women:

> *Young woman from Tucumán sentenced to 8 years in prison for an alleged abortion in Hospital Avellaneda.*
> *A 27-year-old woman was charged, tried, and sentenced to 8 years in prison for miscarrying in the hospital. After awaiting trial in remand for more than 2 years, this week the young woman was ruled against by Chamber III of the Criminal Division of the Supreme Court of Tucumán, composed of three male judges—Dante Ibáñez, Néstor Macoritto, and Fabián Fradejas.*

This is how the press release about the case opens.

> *Justice was far from helpful.*
> *While admitted to a public hospital, Belén was detained at*

the request of Fifth Public Prosecutor Washington Dávila. In other words, Belén has not been home since she was admitted to Hospital Avellaneda, having been remanded in prison, where she remains to this day: 2 years and 1 month later.

This is how Celina and Soledad begin to rewrite her story.

27

TIME TO SHARE

It's two a.m. when Celina goes home. She's planning to send the press release out at eight the next morning, as the radio starts broadcasting the news. Her news agency is far from one of the most widely read media outlets in the region and survives thanks only to the idealistic enthusiasm of its workforce. Plenty of people in Tucumán aren't even aware it exists. The agency is known around poorer neighborhoods because of the community radio stations they set up to teach kids in the area about the industry. The mainstream media has never cited one of its press releases. It doesn't care about the issues and believes the people and incidents in them to be irrelevant. The more widely read news outlets have a clearly marked section for people of the lower classes: the crime notes.

But Celina knows things will be different this time. She figures she should probably get some sleep but quickly gives up on the idea when she crawls into bed. Her brain won't stop humming.

She allows herself to make a small change to the plan she had hatched with Soledad and Sebastián. Instead of sending out the press release at eight a.m., she will send it at four a.m. That way, she can get at least two hours of sleep. She posts it on her Facebook page at five. Ten minutes later, someone shares it. Then another. And another. It's not even six a.m., and dozens of people have already shared the press release. Who cares if she barely got any sleep?

By eight a.m., Celina is at the agency with her colleagues. The website traffic and Facebook engagement is out of control. Just reading the comments isn't enough. They want to know where the readers are based.

Tucumán, Amsterdam, Buenos Aires, London, Córdoba, Copenhagen, Santa Cruz, Madrid, Misiones, Chicago, La Pampa, and Berlin. She keeps checking the map as the news spreads like an undeterrable virus.

Página 12 and *La Nación* are the only Argentine newspapers that pick up the release, though they tell a different story. The *La Nación* headline reads: "Tucumán: Woman Convicted for Killing Her Baby Claims Miscarriage." The paper's Tucumán correspondent notes a plunger was found in the bathroom. Why he made up that detail remains a mystery to this day. Not even the people who misrepresented the case mentioned a plunger.

Tucumán's primary media outlets, including its main newspaper, *La Gaceta*, say nothing. Not that day or any of the days after. They remain silent.

28

CELINA

Celina doesn't have a lot of free time these days. After several attempts, I finally manage to schedule a meeting with her in Tucumán during the Easter holidays.

I make it to the hotel—avoiding the Holy Week procession that starts at Plaza Independencia, outside the Tucumán Government Palace, and ends at the cathedral—after a long walk through a city with street names and monuments that grab my attention. All are men, mostly generals and holy men. There are a lot of battles. The one woman with the privilege of having a street named after her is the Virgin of Mercy. And the only statue of a woman is of the beloved singer Mercedes Sosa. It is caged in the tourist office.

Celina is waiting for me at a terrace bar across from the square. She orders a grilled ham-and-cheese sandwich, and I get a slice of chocolate and dulce de leche cake. She laughs about the fact that the two of us are meeting on Good Friday, when people are supposed to be resting, and mentions she's had a steady, full-time job for a while now. Even though she's young, you can tell she is tired. In the last couple of years, she's ended a relationship, changed jobs, changed activist groups, and taken on debt. She doesn't know what it means to go on vacation. "I've done amazing work the last few years, but I need a break," she says, though I know it isn't true. Celina doesn't slow down or take breaks.

Before broaching the subject that has brought us there that day, I mention the statues of men and the street names. She opens her eyes wide and says: "Careful." She surprises me. "What you're saying is true, but there's always been an important resistance movement in Tucumán—people rose up when the factories closed and during the dictatorship, then there's the women's movement, too. That's why so many of our rallies start at Lola Mora's *Liberty* statue. Tucumán is more than just authoritarian rule. On the other side, there is resistance. That's why we're still here. Lola Mora is from Tucumán, too."

Celina visited Belén in prison several times—with Soledad and also with a representative who came all the way from Buenos Aires to see her. "I walked around the prison with her. The representative greeted all the women in there with a kiss. But when we got to the women who killed the teacher, I couldn't go on. I stayed with Belén, who kept her distance from them, too," she says.

She tells me about her visits to the prison. When articles about the case started coming out, she went on Belén's Facebook page to check for any compromising posts. She felt a mix of relief and anger when she saw the last thing Belén had posted, five days before her hospital visit: a picture of her looking happy, with no belly. No one had bothered to notice that small detail before convicting her.

She confesses to crying every time she said goodbye to Belén. She couldn't stand that she got to go home while Belén had to stay in prison, behind bars.

I found out later that Celina borrowed money so she could employ Belén at her house after she was released from prison. It was basically an excuse to ensure Belén earned a small salary. It's not easy to find work with a criminal record, even if you're innocent.

Celina. She's given Belén a lot more than just the four months it took to get her out. They stayed in contact afterward, and Celina did all she could to help her. Most of the work she was involved in around that time had to do with righting that injustice and countless others.

At some point amid all that, she lost a lot of money and went into debt. She still works more than one job and is currently saving up to go on vacation. She'd like to visit Barcelona one day.

She spends weekends in Amaicha del Valle, an Indigenous community in the Calchaquí Valley, thirty-two miles from Tafí. During the conquest, the Amaicha people did not take part in the war against the Spanish conquistadors. In return, their right to settle on ancestral land was memorialized in a 1716 royal decree. They invoke this document to uphold their status as a community and their ancestral institutions, like the Caciquedom and Elders Council. "Amaicha is my home in the world. It's where I'm able to relax, the only place where the weight on my shoulders seems to lift. I also do some great sleep therapy there. I don't get a lot of sleep in San Miguel [de Tucumán]," she says, nostalgic and resigned.

We hug goodbye.

29

GROUNDLESS

The morning in court when the judges read her the grounds for her conviction, Belén cries again. Unlike the day her verdict was read, the courthouse is packed, because now people in Tucumán know what is happening. There are women's rights and human rights organizations like the National Campaign for Abortion, representatives from Pan y Rosas, the Latin American and Caribbean Committee for the Defense of Women's Rights (CLADEM), and Mumalá (Women of the Latin American Motherland), as well as journalists.

Belén has been summoned, but no one will see her. Instead of calling her to the bench to read the grounds, Soledad has asked for notice to be given to the mayor's office so that Belén won't have to face the cameras. They do exactly this, and Belén waits in handcuffs to hear the reason she was found guilty.

She doesn't want to read her grounds for conviction. She trusts Soledad and would prefer not to relive those accusations.

Striking affirmations are made in the grounds, which describes a scene you wouldn't even expect to see in a horror movie. "That after she gave birth to her son, she cut the umbilical cord, tied it into a knot, and then with calculated impunity and the clear intent to cause the death of her son—at the time in a state of complete vulnerability—threw him into the toilet bowl of the bathroom in the aforementioned hospital and flushed, causing the traumatic brain injury that led to the child's death."

The judges had woven a similar tale in the case of Romina Tejerina, a young woman from Jujuy who was sentenced to fourteen years in prison for killing her newborn daughter after carrying to term a pregnancy resulting from rape. A mix of intellectual and judicial laziness, added to a perspective biased by the social classes of judger and judged, and certain similarities between Belén and Romina—class vulnerability, skin color, a bathroom, an unwanted pregnancy—led the judges to equate the two. The difference is that Belén was convicted without evidence. There was no materiality of the facts, as it is known in legal jargon. They blamed her for something that simply did not happen. There was never an actual baby.

With the grounds for conviction in Soledad's possession, Belén leaves without being seen. Once she is in the police van, she ducks to hide her face. She knows the press is there and that if they get a photo, her father will see her, as will their neighbors. She stays hidden until Paula, the prison guard, whispers: "Calm down, no one can see you anymore. Now raise your head and look outside. All these people are here for you." Belén sits up, at first fearfully. Finally, Belén relaxes. She cries, but this time it's different.

30

A BOOMING SILENCE
IN TUCUMÁN

Belén's incarceration starts making national news. But Tucumán remains silent for another ten days. Not only does *La Gaceta*, the city's primary multimedia platform, have a special relationship with the powers that be, but it has also been known to ban the use of certain words. This is how journalists were prevented from writing the word "dictatorship." "Instead of 'dictatorship,' write 'National Reorganization Process,'" the editors in chief informed their editors and columnists, thereby declaring themselves members of the military junta that formed a dictatorship in a country where thousands upon thousands of men and women were disappeared between 1976 and 1983. Some of the most vicious acts took place in Tucumán.

A similar policy was applied to the word "abortion." It couldn't be written. What isn't written does not exist. When in doubt, use the word "homicide." This didn't happen all that long ago. In 2016, when Belén's case first came to light, omitting the existence of abortions was part of *La Gaceta*'s unwritten style guide.

The newspaper was silent on the issue. The same couldn't be said of its managing editor, Federico Turpe, who posted on Twitter:

"The ignorance on social media is alarming. The reason Belén wasn't convicted for an abortion is that there was none. People will be speechless when they read the grounds for conviction on Tuesday."

But in 2016, people in Tucumán and everywhere else in the world also read news portals. On Sunday, *Infobae*, one of the most widely read news sites in the country and in Latin America, announces that the National Campaign for Abortion will be marching to Casa de la Provincia de Tucumán in Buenos Aires to demand Belén's freedom.

It's becoming harder and harder to pretend nothing is happening. The news finally makes *La Gaceta*'s website:

> *Women's organizations march to Casa de la Provincia de Tucumán demanding freedom for Belén, who has been in prison for more than two years for a spontaneous abortion.*

Celina reads the article and feels energized. She sends it to Soledad, Luli, and Noelia on WhatsApp. Also to Sebastián. But none of them are happy about it. She clicks on the link again and is dumbstruck. They changed the headline, virtually the entire text. The headline in *La Gaceta* now reads:

> **Women's Organizations March to Demand Freedom**
> **for Young Woman Who Murdered Newborn Baby**

The truth had lasted less than fifteen minutes online.

The following Tuesday, after the grounds are read, *La Gaceta* speaks about the case for the first time, basing itself entirely on the grounds for the conviction.

La Gaceta's Federico Turpe takes to Twitter again:

"They tried to pass off a murder as a miscarriage. Worse yet, they used the lie for political ends."

31

CONFIDENTIALITY

In medical school, besides learning about general surgery, anatomy, and other specializations, students are also taught about doctor-patient confidentiality. Not only is it sanctioned by law in Argentina, but it is also part of the foundation of trust patients place in the medical professionals who attend to them. Doctor-patient confidentiality dates as far back as the Hippocratic oath, in which physicians swear to "keep silent about anything I see or hear, whether inside or outside the examination room, that pertains to the lives of men and ought not to be disclosed. I will keep secret anything that may prove shameful if it were to become known."

This professional confidentiality is covered in the code of medical ethics of the Buenos Aires National Academy of Medicine. Its violation is punishable by the Criminal Code of Argentina. Professional confidentiality is also written into the Criminal Procedure Code of Tucumán Province. It exists for the reason that if a person fears their doctor will report them for whatever caused their medical condition, they may be discouraged from disclosing information that is paramount to their treatment. Human life is valued above all else, at least in democratic states.

Belén was denied professional confidentiality from the get-go. A policewoman entered the room where she was being examined, interrupted her examination, and interrogated the doctor, who didn't hesitate to tell the policewoman that his patient was experiencing a miscarriage. Minutes earlier, he'd been writing "miscarriage" in her medical records. But faced with the policewoman's account that a fetus had been found in the hospital bathroom, he didn't contest her depiction of events. He provided biased information to a person whose job is to prosecute criminal offenses. And in 2014 Argentina, induced abortions were a criminal offense. As they continue to be in 2019, at the time of our story.

The policewoman, who knew nothing about medicine or the law, decided Belén had committed murder. This is how absurd the whole thing was. And she is the reason this is in the medical record, which is property of the patient. In this case, Belén. Belén's story is no longer her own. It is the story that others, who decided she was a murderer, wrote for her.

The book *Jaque a la reina*, which Soledad gave to Belén, features research she conducted with Mariana Álvarez and Alejandra Iriarte that involved surveying trial courts across Tucumán Province. It is surprising to find that prosecutors in Tucumán not only investigate induced abortions, or abortions leading to death, but also spontaneous abortions or miscarriages. As of 2014, there was still a great deal of confusion about the criminal status of abortions. By handing over information about Belén's miscarriage to a member of law enforcement, the medical staff put the patient's diagnosis in the hands of a person who is trained to suppress crime.

32

IN SEARCH OF A REASON

I'm still as surprised as everyone who has learned and will continue to learn about this case. How could it be?

We're talking about a miscarriage.

I decide to do some reading. I immerse myself in the book *Malas madres, aborto e infanticidio en perspectiva histórica* (Bad mothers, abortion, and infanticide: A historical perspective) by Julieta Di Corleto, a lawyer with ample research background in women and Argentine criminal law.

I think I've found some answers here. The book looks at cases of women accused of murdering their children. "The refuge of male dominance and the discourses of lawyers, judges, and other legal practitioners reintroduce old forms of legal production. By this, I don't mean to suggest that legal frameworks are immutable so much as put forward the idea that the law does not operate independently. Both its strength and its efficacy rest on legal practitioners and on the contexts that shield them, which are oftentimes resistant to change."

In other words, a law's mere existence does not necessarily mean it will always be observed by those involved in the judicial process.

Personal beliefs and the roles imposed on us also play a crucial role when it comes to judging women—at least in the cases Di Corleto examines in her doctoral thesis.

Norma Bulacio, Belén's public defender, was also useful to those who held the dominant discourse. She, too, chose to base her defense strategy on another bias that gets foisted on women: insanity. For a long time, postpartum depression was considered a mood disorder. Any woman who fails at motherhood is somehow at fault, whether or not the pregnancy was wanted, forced, or unwanted. And in the context of a classist, patriarchal, biased society, this failure makes women criminals, insane, or both at the same time.

At that time in Argentina, it wasn't only induced abortions, punishable by law, that were persecuted.

One thing that surprised me enormously when I started researching this book is that Tucumán doesn't only prosecute abortions that are not covered by the exceptions written in the Criminal Code. The city also prosecutes both legal abortions and miscarriages—that is, the loss of a pregnancy because the fetus has stopped growing or developing normally. According to the study conducted by Soledad Deza, Alejandra Iriarte, and Mariana Álvarez, which was referenced in *Jaque a la reina* and cited by Soledad before Congress, 24 percent of the suits filed against women in Tucumán since 2008 correspond to adverse obstetric outcomes. In other words, spontaneous abortions or miscarriages. "These trials end up being more moral than legal," the authors write.

Out of the 79 percent of the five hundred women whose cases were archived, only 1 percent had their charges dismissed. That is, only five women had their criminal cases closed. The criminal cases against the rest of the women remain open, meaning that their criminal record would show there is a pending case against them.

In other words, in many places across Argentina, a woman's failure to choose motherhood, whatever the reason, instantly makes her a criminal.

Is it because of a lack of education? The patriarchy? Or because of a legal and judicial system devised and controlled by men who belong to a social class that feels secure enough to cause pregnancies while also washing their hands of them?

During one of my many trips to Tucumán, I decide to visit Tafí del Valle, a dreamy region on the Tucumán side of the Calchaquí Valley—the lesser-known, almost hidden, yet nonetheless magical side of the valley. It's circled by hills and sky. At someone's recommendation, I go for a walk on a trail cluttered with empty houses. Several people mention these beautiful houses, which are empty from February to December. "Did you go see the empty houses?" a mountain guide asks me just as we've switched from talking about the landscape to talking about the myths around legal abortion in Tucumán. "Yes, they're very pretty," I reply. "The houses fill up in December because the capital becomes incredibly hot, while here, in Tafí del Valle, the weather is perfect. Mild in the daytime and cool at night. Lots of teenagers and young people from well-to-do families travel here from the capital. They go out with girls in the area and aren't careful. By end of summer, dozens of girls are pregnant. But the boys and their families leave just as easily as they came," the guide tells me, and for a moment, all we can do is stand there in silence.

On the way back, I tell myself I will keep looking for answers.

33

WOMEN IN ACTION

Women's organizations across Tucumán Province are on alert.

Some are from left-wing parties, many from human rights groups, and others from women's rights activist groups. Together they create the Provincial Organization to Free Belén as a way to bring together everyone who wants to collaborate on the cause. They need to concentrate efforts and get organized. They will have to face the Tucumán judicial system and government, as well as the Catholic and evangelical churches, which they know are not on their side. The media, too. Their one goal is to free Belén. This is how Catholics for Choice, the Fundación Mujeres x Mujeres, the National Campaign for Abortion, Casa de las Mujeres Norma Nassif, Mumalá, and Pan y Rosas members join forces with labor unions and representatives of left-wing political parties. Besides the convictions and independent advocacy efforts of a few representatives, abortion is not currently a nonpartisan issue. As months pass, this will begin to change.

The meetings range from passionate speeches to exchanges with lawyers. It isn't long before the women begin to truly understand and incorporate into their lexicon phrases and legal terms that help substantiate their public discussions about women's rights in general and Belén's rights in particular: "due process," "breach of professional confidentiality," "pretrial detention that does not meet human rights standards," "a negligent public defender," and "inconsistent evidence."

The desire to fight for Belén's freedom imposes order on the chaos of the organization's first meeting. A schedule is laid out, including a press conference, a call to action, awareness-raising activities, and integrating the fight for Belén's freedom into the one-year anniversary of the first major #NiUnaMenos demonstration.

Yanina Muñoz, an activist from the Mumalá group, requests the floor.

"Compañeras. The Mumalá group is going to wear masks like we did during Marita Verón's trial. Because we are all Belén."

Everyone applauds.

The first march for Belén's freedom is scheduled for May 28, 2016, the International Day of Action for Women's Health. It is an especially cold and rainy day in Tucumán, and the women march from the courthouse to Plaza Independencia.

Besides masks, the Mumalá women also bring PVC pipes to represent prison bars. Some women wear the bandanas from the National Campaign for Abortion, a symbol others are seeing for the first time in their lives.

> *Freedom for Belén!*
> *Sex ed so we can decide!*
> *Contraceptives avoid abortions!*
> *Legalize abortion! Save lives!*

When Soledad, Noelia, and Luli arrive at the meeting point, they are surprised to find a group of women gathered in front of the courthouse. They wonder if another march had been planned for that day. Then the women unfurl a banner that says FREEDOM FOR BELÉN. It acts as a kind of beacon. The group they didn't recognize is composed of women who'd come to demand freedom for Belén after hearing about the protest.

I remember a phrase I once heard from the feminist sociologist Dora Barrancos: "When I go somewhere and see unfamiliar faces, I instantly realize our numbers are growing."

The photographers covering the protest are intrigued by a young pregnant woman marching under the cold rain. They take a photo of her. Her name is Fernanda Doz Costa. An employee of Amnesty International, Fernanda had worked at the headquarters in London up until a few months ago. Then, wanting her children to be born in her home province and to have family nearby, she put in a request to work remotely from a small town in Tucumán Province.

Fernanda's cell phone rings, and she takes cover under the awning of a bar. It's London, so she wants to take the call right away.

"Hi, Fernanda, are you from the same Tucumán as Belén?" a voice asks her.

"Yes, I'm at the march right now."

"Let's do everything we can to get her out."

"Yes, of course," Fernanda replies and then keeps walking under the rain while chanting, "Freedom for Belén."

34

FROM SILENCE TO THE UN

In Argentina, as in many places the world over, you have to make noise outside the country so that people at home will hear about it.

Mariela Belski, the executive director of Amnesty International, and Paola García Rey, a lawyer for the organization, know this. Which is why they decide to call Victoria Donda, president of the Argentine Chamber of Deputies' Human Rights and Guarantees Committee.

"We need to organize an event to get Juan Méndez [then the United Nations' special rapporteur on torture] over here. If we can't convince someone from outside the country to come to Argentina, I don't think people in the country will ever get involved."

"Don't worry. I'll take care of it."

That same afternoon, Paula invites Méndez to attend a conference she and her colleagues just thought of, called: "The Role of the State in Matters of Gender-Based Violence: Torture and Ill-Treatment in the World of Sexual Reproduction and Health." The rapporteur immediately replies to say he will come to Buenos Aires to attend the conference.

Soledad Deza and Fernanda Doz Costa travel from Tucumán to Buenos Aires for the conference. On the morning of May 19, they meet with the rapporteur in the Amnesty Argentina offices on Calle Paraguay. The cold is a good incentive for them to get lunch at El Globo, which serves one of the best puchero stews in the area. Soledad sits strategically next to Juan and begins telling him about the Belén case. Juan has lived in Washington, DC, for years, but he was born and raised in Argentina. He can't believe there is a woman in prison for abortion in his home country. Neither Soledad nor Juan takes a single bite of food.

"I'd prepared a presentation about reproductive rights in Argentina. But I changed the focus of the presentation. It was imperative that we do something for Belén," he would tell me later.

"Women and children are subjected to multiple forms of violence, both in the field of sexual and reproductive rights and by way of laws, policies, and state practices aimed at controlling their lives and their bodies," Méndez said that afternoon at the Chamber of Deputies. "When the state perpetuates discriminatory stereotypes and gender bias, it allows illegal acts to be committed and go unpunished. It also fails to fulfill its duty to prevent gender-based violence, torture, and ill treatment."

Paola from Amnesty Argentina pointed out that Belén's case was not an isolated one. "On the contrary, the threat of the penal system hangs over the heads of many other women as a way to intimidate and punish them for not adhering to the model of the reproductive mother. Gender-based violence and the denial of women's sexual and reproductive health is a clear example of political disinterest in protecting and guaranteeing the rights of women and girls."

The tactic works. The media responds to the call to interview UN representative Juan Méndez.

"The case interests me. It aligns with the types of cases we've been examining. Many women who try to access health care services or exercise their legal rights are met with discriminatory and patriarchal behavior, which constitutes cruel, inhumane treatment."

Juan Méndez requests more information on the case so he can evaluate if Belén's human rights were violated and if a complaint should be filed against the government of Argentina, forcing it to issue an explanation.

By the next day, news has spread beyond *Página 12*. *Infobae* writes, "UN: A Total Ban on Abortion Violates Convention Against Torture," and publishes Juan Méndez's statements about the Belén case.

Federal and state offices from Buenos Aires to Tucumán take note: the case is now on the United Nations' radar.

35

#NIUNAMENOS: NOT ONE LESS

June 3, 2016, marks one year since the #NiUnaMenos march. That first year, the call for a protest began with a tweet that a journalist, Marcela Ojeda, posted shortly after news came out of another femicide: fourteen-year-old Chiara Páez had been murdered in Rufino in the Santa Fe province. A group of journalists, media experts, and activists quickly came together to shape the march, whose primary slogans were #NiUnaMenos (Not One Less) and #BastadeFemicidios (No More Femicides).

The issue of illegal abortions had come up in previous organizational meetings and was considered a brutal form of violence against women. However, the organizers decided to broaden the focus of the protest to include femicide and gender-based violence more generally. At the time, these subjects were totally absent from political discourse and the public agenda, outside a small pool of activists and feminist journalists.

Yet the document that would be read at the main Congressional Plaza event in 2015, which featured authors, journalists, actresses, and screenwriters—like Ingrid Beck, Marina Abiuso, Hinde Pomeraniec, Marcela Ojeda, Micaela Libson, Florencia Etcheves, Soledad Vallejos, Valeria Sampedro, Mercedes Funes, Marta Dillon, Florencia Minici, Gabriela Cabezón Cámara, Florencia Alcaraz, among others—included the following:

This is why we reassert our right to say no *to something we don't want, whether it's a partner, a pregnancy, sex, or a traditional way of life. We reassert our right to say* no *to the social mandates of submission and obedience. And saying* no *to these things means we can say yes to our bodies, our emotional lives, our sexuality, to our participation in society, work, politics, and everywhere else.*

The document underscored the importance of making headway in legalizing and decriminalizing abortion. Actors Juan Minujín and Érica Rivas and cartoonist Maitena read the full proclamation wearing a green bandana stamped with the words LEGAL, SAFE, AND FREE ABORTION around their necks.

Rereading that document, I realize that we make the same claims about the way femicides and domestic violence cases are treated as we do about the way victims of abuse and illegal abortions are treated.

The way most of the media addresses this problem has to change. Too often, victims are blamed for their fates: their clothes, their friends, how they have fun. Deep down, the press fans the idea that "they brought it on themselves." We need a news media that is committed to creating new protocols while adhering to existing protocols and codes of ethics when covering cases like these. Television reproduces words and images that put women in situations of danger, inequality, and dominance. It reproduces stereotypes. When women and girls who fall victim to violence are covered by the media, their private lives are trespassed.

I remember the image of reporters from channel 8 pushing their way toward the car the day Belén was released. And Belén's insistence on keeping her identity secret, from the very beginning. Neither Belén nor Soledad let the press harass her family and friends. Fighting to protect Belén's private life was a way of shielding her from more violence.

"The press wouldn't leave me alone," Belén reminds me every time we see each other. "In the end the justice system said I was innocent. So why do some people still believe my family and I are guilty of something?"

"This massive show of excitement, this widespread, committed social participation, are a unanimous cry. Not One Less," the 2015 document ends.

A year later, the demands on behalf of femicide victims would be joined by countrywide calls for Belén's freedom.

36

BELÉN MEETS MARÍA MAGDALENA

In prison, people start calling her Belén. Her name isn't the only thing that has changed. She, too, is different. The chapter about the María Magdalena case that Soledad wrote about in *Jaque a la reina*, the book she gave Belén the first day they met, is one Belén knows almost by heart.

"I've underlined the whole book," she tells me. "The same exact thing happened to me. I remember I wrote loads of letters about how there were more cases like mine. I sent one to my mom. I wrote to Soledad about all the similarities I found in the book."

In her letters, she points out why everything she went through was unjust. She'd write, and the guilt that had been forced on her rolled down the paper until it evaporated. To the other inmates, she has become famous. "People are going to start asking you for autographs," her cellmate Vanessa is always telling her.

Everyone in the cellblock eagerly awaits the news bulletin. They want to hear updates about the case. They like seeing how people on the outside describe what's happening inside prison walls.

Soledad and Celina go to prison to update Belén on how things are going. Suddenly the press wants to talk to her, but the three of them agree they should wait.

They tell her there will be a #NiUnaMenos demonstration, and that the protesters are going to demand her freedom. And they give her the letters from women who've started writing to her to say she isn't alone, women who tell her they are going to march for her freedom.

37

BLINDSIDED

Soledad's old life is on hold. Her day-to-day with her husband and two children is now a space of mutual support. Although Soledad has always been a whirlwind of enthusiasm and emotional support, she begins to lose heart. She'd promised Belén freedom and can't bring herself to let her down. This is the closest Soledad has ever been to such a huge miscarriage of justice, and she has more than just the powerful and legal sectors of a patriarchal society in her sights—the image of Belén's crying face asking for help is also burned into her memory. When it all becomes too much, she lights a cigarette and gazes up at the sky from her patio. When she sits back down at her computer, she puts her hair in a bun. She says it helps her think.

She decides to set aside everything but her classes at the university and the movie marathons she and her family have on Sundays. Her husband and children indulge her when she repeatedly suggests watching a movie featuring a strong-willed female lead, and, more than once, Soledad's husband, son, and daughter compare her to the character. "She doesn't stop until justice is served."

Florencia, Soledad's youngest child, also loves these movie marathons. She's still young and has only recently started wondering about feminism and whether it's something she wants to be part of. The question isn't top of mind for most of the girls at her high school.

But it hurts Florencia to see her mother crying and asking to be left alone—she just needs a minute.

Florencia's calm, cheerful demeanor changes one morning when a student announces in class: "Florencia's mom is defending a murderer." Florencia feels angry, and a new energy shoots through the calm and quiet of a girl who's grown up with the solution to all her immediate problems at her fingertips. Soledad is her idol, and Belén is innocent. Her rage doesn't compromise her focus. She stands in front of her classmates and Spanish teacher and says: "My mother is defending a woman who was unjustly imprisoned. She isn't a murderer. She was incarcerated for being poor, and because no one listened to her. She's in prison for having a miscarriage. She's innocent, and my mom is going to help get her released." Then she sits back down and tries to hide how upset she is. Her big, tanned cheeks are pure fire. In the ensuing silence, everyone in the classroom looks at each other. Until the teacher says: "Tell your mom kudos from me. What she's doing is very important." Florencia smiles again. She has decided to be a feminist.

38

ARGENTINA, TOO

In Buenos Aires, women's human rights organizations plan their actions. The National Campaign for Abortion, the Center for Legal and Social Studies, and Catholics for Choice reach out to their networks and ask them to join the fight for Belén's freedom.

Amnesty International initiates an urgent action, something it calls "a solidarity strategy." The action urges authorities to immediately release Belén and ensure her physical and mental integrity. It calls on them to investigate the health professionals who infringed on doctor-patient confidentiality in order to ascertain who is at fault. It urges authorities to ensure safe and legal abortions for girls and women, these being necessary to their health and well-being.

Amnesty Argentina posts a series of images on Twitter that say:

> *She had a miscarriage.*
> *They showed her a fetus in the hospital.*
> *They told her, "This is your son."*
> *This counts as torture.*
> *Now she's in prison.*
> *#FreedomForBelén*

Amnesty International Hong Kong director Mabel Au Mei-po writes to Mariela Belski to say a demonstration will be held in Taiwan. The same will happen in the United Kingdom, Spain, Germany, and several other countries. The urgent action for Belén becomes one of Amnesty Argentina's most successful internationally.

The result is more than 120,000 signatures from places as far-flung as Taiwan—the country that garnered the most signatures—Belgium, the United Kingdom, Portugal, and New Zealand, among others. "The world is paying attention to Argentina. It's time for the authorities to listen, for justice to be served, and for Belén to go free," said Mariela Belski.

> Belén, you're not alone.
> Chin up, Belén, we're with you.
> We're fighting for you and for women who've been unjustly incarcerated all over the world.
> I'm writing to you as a sister from the other side of the world.

These are some of the messages Belén receives in letters and on postcards. Some—many of them—include drawings, since the senders assume Belén may not understand their language.

This is how she came to be surrounded by images of hearts and the silhouettes of hugging women and girls.

Why was there such an overwhelming global response to Amnesty International's urgent action?

"Because no one thought things like this happened in Argentina. They thought El Salvador was the only place in Latin America where women could go to prison for abortion," Fernanda Doz Costa tells me when I ask.

At least eighteen women have been imprisoned for abortion in El Salvador since the exceptions decriminalizing abortion were struck in 1998. The country has some of the most restrictive abortion laws in the world.

39

MIND THE GAP

Aileen is nineteen years old and lives in London. She takes the tube to Victoria Station every day for work. One day she finds a discarded issue of *Metro* on the seat next to hers, with a full-page Amnesty International ad that reads:

URGENT ACTION: FREE BELÉN
JAILED FOR A MISCARRIAGE

She puts the newspaper into her backpack and takes it out again when she gets to work. She sends an email adding her name to the petition. Hers was one of 52,000 signatures collected in the United Kingdom.

That afternoon, she writes a letter:

"Belén, you are not alone. Your freedom is our freedom." Then she draws a woman flexing her biceps.

40

THE JUDGES ARE SMOKING AND DRINKING COFFEE IN THEIR CHAMBERS

Letters and chocolates start streaming into the prison. The prison staff read the letters first and also cut into the chocolates. Breaking open food sent to prisoners is one part of mail inspection. This is why Belén doesn't want anyone sending her empanadas. "I mean, who wants to eat a crumbled empanada?" she will say later. She doesn't mind so much with the chocolates. She just asks them not to destroy the packaging so she can keep it as a memento.

A lot of people want to see Belén, but she prefers to keep visits to a minimum.

Celina explains to Belén and her lawyers that it is extremely important for her to express everything she lived through and is still living through in her own words. They're going to make the most of next week's visit from Paola García Rey.

Belén accepts. Her first interview will be conducted by Celina for APA.

Here is an excerpt from that piece:

Belén recalls that first day Soledad came to prison. . . . "I was guilty, a murderer. She came, and now I'm like this. Yesterday when I was talking to my mom on the phone, she had me listen to news reports about the case on TV, and to the public prosecutor's opinion. I asked them to turn up the volume and cried as I listened.

"My sister is a pillar for my parents. My mom and my dad. I was scared the trial would break her. I thought about her all the time. We used to fight a lot when we were kids, about silly things, but then we became really close. She had an anxiety attack the day of the trial, and I was so scared for her.

"I think the public prosecutor is right: the doctors were behaving like judges, like attorneys, like police officers."

When she gets the signs and letters from Amnesty, her face lights up, and Paola tells her: "There are a lot of us waiting for you to get out."

Again, Belén says, "I can't believe it. I'm still standing, despite everything. I don't know what would've happened if [Soledad] hadn't shown up here." She cries. "It may be easy to get in, but it's hard to get out."

"I always cry on the phone with my mom."

As she looks at the letters scrawled in different languages from different places and covered in drawings, she says: "This kind of thing can make a person whole." She calls over one of the prison guards and asks her for a bottle of water. She feels overwhelmed.

"They're good to me here, and they've always stood by me, even when I was at my worst: the day of my sentencing, the day my caption was changed, that day was awful."

She shows the prison guard everything she's been brought—signs, letters. The prison guard jokes: "With all this support, I'd let you out myself."

"I'll never forget the people who stood by me when I most needed it, throughout the trial; I will never forget it—there was a day when I couldn't stop sobbing."

The guard says Belén kept yelling, "Why am I here?" It was August 21, 2015, the day her caption was changed. The guard tells me that female corrections officers are discriminated against, too. "If you make a mistake, they say it's because you're a woman, they say, 'You women don't know how to work.' In here, we have to be therapists, friends, mothers; we live here. Our lives change with the job. When I was a kid, I used to study at a religious school. I never thought I'd be in this line of work. But then I didn't get to finish, because my dad lost his job, and I found myself working in this place. I also came to believe that there were no bad people here. I started spending time with other inmates and guards, and realized we all suffer the same discriminations. No one is born a prison guard; the longer you're here, the more the uniform molds to you, though I guess it depends on the person. Our low prison population means we know who everyone is. If there's a problem, we know their mother, their father, their life story. Belén is the first woman we've had here for an abortion.

"On October 17, 2014, Belén asked me to talk to her lawyer [Musi]. She asked me to call him because he wasn't showing up. She never had good counsel. Ever."

"Even though my mom was with me at the hospital the whole time, they never asked her to testify, because they said she'd be charged as an accomplice," Belén continues. "My family showed my public defender some photographs of me from a few days before—before I went to the hospital. In the photos, I don't have a belly. I'm wearing a tank top. They never bothered to put them in evidence, and when I was convicted my mom asked the lawyer to give the photos back. She never showed her face here again. Throughout the process, people kept saying, 'You'll get out next month, you'll get out next month.' But nothing happened.

"When I saw the appeal for cassation I just couldn't believe it. That was the first time I showed my sister any legal documents, and when she saw all the mistakes that had been made, she said, 'I can't believe it.' I'm so grateful to everyone who's been sending me strength. Looking at all this, I feel speechless. At first I used to wonder: How are they going to talk about it on TV? It's embarrassing. I'm the only idiot who got thrown behind bars for a miscarriage."

About the doctors and lawyers, Belén says: "The doctors who accused me are still living their lives. The men who convicted me get to go on like nothing happened. And I'm still in here. All I'm asking is for them to reevaluate the case. They don't know what it's like waking up in the same place every day, being away from your family every day. They're in their homes. They don't know what it's like to have to file a request just to see a friend."

The judges are in their chambers, smoking, drinking coffee. And they have to live with the fact that they sentenced me to this place. What happened to me happened because I couldn't get hold of 20,000 pesos in less than forty-eight hours. If I'd had the money, I could've defended myself. But I thought: Why should I have to pay money when I did nothing wrong?

I'm going to get out of here one day. I'm going to get out to fight for my rights, to be with my family. I heard some women are scared of going to the hospital with a hemorrhage (I say that if they go to a clinic they'll be fine, but if they go to a public hospital they may wind up in prison), and I say don't be scared. We have to fight so that this never happens again. I want the doctors to lose their licenses, for their salaries to be docked for the years I served in prison, so they know what it's like not to have money. Now everyone in the justice system is aware of my case, and I'm still here, far away from my family, who I only get to see twice a week. They weren't in this situation when they pointed all ten of their fingers at me. They tortured me, made me look at a black thing like this, the size of a hand, lying in a box. They sentenced me and then they washed their hands. Now I want them to fix it.

41

THROUGH MY FAULT, THROUGH MY MOST GRIEVOUS FAULT

The year 2016 is Argentina's bicentennial, and the government of Tucumán is deciding on the many activities that will take place throughout the various festivities. The first is the Eleventh National Eucharistic Congress, which will be held in Tucumán Province, with Pope Francis attending, although when the time comes, the Argentine Pope sends an Italian cardinal, Giovanni Battista Re, as his representative instead.

Governor Juan Manzur of Tucumán Province is excited about the celebration. "Two hundred years ago today, Argentina was born in Tucumán. From that day on, we've been free. More than thirty-three percent of the delegates were Catholic. This means the church was there with us when we shouted 'Freedom.'"

Belén hears about this because the women in the prison have been tasked with fixing up the place in case anyone comes to visit them. She enjoys painting and is excited to do it, even though it's cold in the yard when it's her turn to paint the walls.

There is an uproar on social media when female journalists in Tucumán learn they won't be allowed to cover the Eucharistic Congress. Spokespeople for the Vatican take to Twitter to request that press access to an event with government authorities and the pa-

pal legate be restricted to men "in dress pants, a dress shirt, tie, and blazer." Rosalía Cazorla is one of the loudest voices on social media, calling out what she feels to be discrimination. The Eucharistic Congress replies to her on Twitter: "It's not discrimination. By Episcopal Orders, Cardinal Re can only be accompanied by men."

The ensuing scandal is so great—and only a year after #Ni UnaMenos—that the congress quickly decides to let women into the event. "It was an error of interpretation," a spokesperson close to the cardinal offers as clarification and then immediately deletes the previous tweet.

The governor and important political figures in Tucumán are euphoric that people are flocking to their city. President Mauricio Macri and Vice President Gabriela Michetti fly in from Buenos Aires. Senator Silvia Elías de Pérez, who in two years' time will fiercely oppose the bill to legalize abortion, tweets ecstatically about her participation in the signing of an agreement between the politicians and the bishops.

The prison staff are informed that Cardinal Re has asked to take part at the mass scheduled at the penitentiary; the women's allotted downtime and workshop hours are decreased so the inmates can focus on cleaning up the building and weeding the yard. The cardinal can't see the prison in a poor state, they're told. The flower murals in the yard aren't enough anymore; they're going to have to paint several images of Christ throughout the penitentiary, with the largest gracing the entrance. It should feel like the prison is somehow part of the Eucharistic Congress.

Belén divides her time between the yard and the kitchen. They have to make pastries and empanadas for the cardinal and his staff.

The day finally comes, and they get the main common area ready for Cardinal Re to give mass. A large poster that says GIVE ME MERCY has been put up in the front. White and yellow flowers are arranged in a vase.

They were very happy to be receiving visitors, especially since they'd get to enjoy some of the food they cooked.

> *O merciful God, forgive them their sins.*
> *Repeat after me: Through my fault, through my most*
>   *grievous fault.*

When the mass ends, Cardinal Re eats a pastry prepared by Belén and the other inmates. At one point, as she is watching him, the delegate asks the warden: "Is this where the *ragazza* Belén is being held?" Belén, who is standing next to him, holding a tray of pastries, stares at the warden and pleads with her eyes for her to preserve her anonymity.

The prisoners remain silent.

"No, Cardinal, Belén isn't here."

"That's a shame. I would've liked to meet her."

The cardinal was joined at the mass by Regino Amado, the Tucumán secretary of state, and Alfredo Zecca, the archbishop of Tucumán.

When they left the prison, Secretary of State Amado spoke to the press: "Cardinal Re brought hope to people incarcerated for various reasons; he offered them the possibility of repentance, reconciliation, and peace with God."

42

WOMEN FROM HERE

Since May 12, 2015, I've developed a close friendship with nine of the journalists who helped plan the first #NiUnaMenos demonstration. Whenever we get ideas in our heads, emotions get high in our group text, which is filled with a strong desire to change the world, contradictions, and a lot of laughter and anxiety.

There's the journalist Marcela Ojeda, who constantly gets appeals for help from female victims of violence and doesn't rest until she finds a way to redress those injustices. And Valeria Sampedro, who is raw power. On the one hand, she makes you cry with laughter. Meanwhile, on TV, she refuses to look away when faced with tough questions and loses her composure only in cases when, for example, an interviewer says an eleven-year-old girl would willingly enter into a sexual relationship with a sixty-year-old man. When it airs on TV her words won't be distorted, although it has become a custom to do that on the news.

Marcela still works as a reporter for Radio Continental and Valeria as a host for Todo Noticias. Together, they have a radio program on Radio Nacional called *Mujeres de acá*, or "Women from Here."

One year after #NiUnaMenos, they invite some of the demonstration's organizers to speak on their program. We mention there's a woman in prison for a miscarriage, and Marcela and Valeria start thinking about how to broach the subject on their next show.

"We have to interview her," Valeria texts Marcela at six the next morning as they're both commuting to work. They're excited about the idea. They make a couple of phone calls and inquiries, then immediately rule it out. They can't take the time off work, and there's no guarantee they'd be able to record her.

Valeria doesn't lose hope and decides to wait until eight that morning to call Soledad Deza. "Hi, listen, Marcela Ojeda and I have a radio program, and we want to interview Belén. I can check with the station about sending a crew to her in the prison," she suggests.

Soledad says it can't be done. Valeria insists, and Soledad wonders what she can give her instead. She knows the prison would never let the radio crew into the building to record the interview.

"I know. I can ask her to write a letter for you to read on the show. Would that work?"

"Yeah! I love that. We can read it on air during our Sunday radio program."

Soledad tells Belén about the request the next time she visits her in prison. "They'll read it on the radio, then we can read it at the next demonstration. What do you think?" she asks. Belén likes the idea. She loves writing. She also wants to thank her supporters. They agree that Celina will pick up the letter in two days, then Soledad leaves.

By the time of her next visit, the letter is done. Belén hides it up the sleeve of her sweater. The prisoners aren't allowed to send out any written material without management reviewing it first, and she's scared they'll change it.

Celina and Belén hold hands while they talk and wait for the right moment to pass the letter from Belén's sweater sleeve to Celina's. Even though they're both nervous, they know they will succeed.

Celina walks out of the penitentiary with the piece of crumpled paper. "Don't send it to them like that. Copy it out nice and neat," Belén tells her.

The show airs on June 19, 2016.

Marcela Ojeda introduces the case.

Valeria reads the letter on air:

Greetings to all the women, to the warriors, and to everyone who's stood by me until now.

I want to thank you for making my fight your own. Thank you for standing up for me, for making sure my voice and truth were heard.

I was silent for two years. I couldn't bring myself to talk. I was scared. They told me I would get life. They convicted me on hearsay alone, for being poor, for going to a public hospital, for not having the money to go to a private clinic and hire a good lawyer.

I haven't been home or seen my family since March 21, 2014. They robbed me of so much. All I wanted was help and instead I was detained, surrounded by police officers and accusatory fingers. Two years and three months away from home. They took away my life!

Did any of them wonder how I felt that night? They accused me and asked if I'd induced an abortion. My mother was mistreated, too. No one cared about me. She's ignorant, she doesn't know anything, they probably told themselves. Even though I said I hadn't done anything, that I hadn't killed anyone. I didn't even know I was pregnant. I cry because of the injustice I'm experiencing. But I'm also calm, because I know I will get justice. I am stronger now, calmer.

I never hurt anyone, never stole, never killed, I don't do drugs. I've worked my whole life. I always did everything I was supposed to.

I will forever be grateful to everyone who's helped my voice be heard. *I'm sending you all my love. It makes me so happy not to be alone.*

Thank you and thank you again to all you women. Let us all fight and be heard so that no woman is imprisoned for abortion again. Now your struggle is my struggle, too.

With all my affection,
Belén

43

MARIANA

The Organization to Free Belén sets up a Facebook page. Amid all the messages of solidarity, there is one concrete offer to help:

Hi. This is Mariana, from Mendoza. I've been following this case a long time! I can't believe what they've done to Belén!! For a while now I've wondered how I can help. I'm a graphic designer, so please keep me in mind for anything you need.

I found out about the Belén case through my dad, who's a doctor. He's devoted his life to women's issues, giving talks at national women's conferences, always studying and thinking about the different problems that some, if not all, of us will unfortunately experience. For my part, I've tried to make sure the visual messaging of his work is clear, so that we're thinking not only of the message but how it's delivered. We've put together talks on obstetric violence, unnecessary c-sections, infant mortality, abortion, etc.

I contact Mariana, and she writes back to me on Facebook, all the way from her new home in Barcelona.

I just called my dad to tell him about your message. I said: "Pa, my story is your story, too, from the day I was born I've been listening, seeing, we read together, and you tell me about these issues." When I read about the Belén case, I was so sad and outraged. I couldn't believe what they'd done to her, what they were doing to her. I started thinking about how I could help from almost 1,000 km away. That's why I wrote that message on Facebook. From then on, I started chatting with Celina and Soledad, who sent me information, and when I got out of work, I'd mock up some proposals for them, we worked night and day for months, I think our collective labor made us stronger and more hopeful every day. The visibility the case was getting made me think we were on the right track, that Belén would get justice and go home soon, and that's all I wanted.

Well, dear Ana, that's my story. I was thinking about how important it is for us to come together around these issues, for us to experience cases like Belén's as our own. No distance is too far, we can't just stand around doing nothing, we have to help each other, to be listened to, to see, and, most of all, believe.

I remember the countless hours I spent with the academic Paola Bergallo—a driving force in the movement to decriminalize abortion in Argentina—thinking about all the invisible work women do and how it can slowly change the course of history. Mariana's name is in the book *Libertad para Belén* (Freedom for Belén) that Soledad wrote a few months after her release. "I want to thank Mariana Cardello, whom I've never met, but who offered to help us all the way from Mendoza the minute she heard about the case."

44

THE RIGHT TO CHOOSE
WHO I TALK TO

The only chair in the clothing stall is next to the curtain that sections off the dressing room. Belén borrows a stool from the stall next door so I can have somewhere to sit.

No one here or in my neighborhood knows I'm Belén. They don't know what happened to me. I think it's better that way, because people are quick to judge. I didn't do anything wrong. Whenever anyone wants to talk about the Belén case, I always ask Soledad to tell me why first. Because one thing Soledad taught me is that I have the right to choose who I talk to. She always helped me with that.

When the cardinal came to prison, I didn't want to speak to him. Because he reminded me of the priest in the hospital who said I was a murderer. I didn't want him to blame me or take photos of me. I baked pastries and cookies for him and the government officials, then I had to serve them the food I'd made. But I already knew by then that no one could make me talk about anything I didn't want to talk about with anyone I didn't want to talk to.

I knew this so deeply that when the secretary of human rights came to visit without letting me know ahead of time, I refused to see him. [Claudio] Avruj was his name. Before Soledad came into my life, no one cared about me. Then people around the world started talking about the case and sending me letters, and suddenly everyone wanted to see me. But I didn't want to be seen. I wanted justice. One afternoon they told me, "The secretary is here." But I hadn't made any plans with him. And they said, "But he's the secretary, you can't say no." I asked to speak with Soledad, and I asked her if he'd been in touch with her, and she was as surprised as I was. "Do I have to see him? He didn't ask if I wanted him to visit." And she said, "No, honey. Remember, no one can make you do something you don't want to." So I won't see him. I don't know why he's here. They have to understand that what I think counts for something, too.

45

THE REPUBLIC OF WOMEN FROM TUCUMÁN

"Are you really going to interview Gioconda Belli? Please tell her how important she was to me," Belén says. "When I read *The Republic of Women*, I told all the girls in prison about the story. I said, 'Look at how these women got organized. What the book said is true, a world run by men is never going to believe us or give us a seat at the table. We need to figure out how to get organized and create a republic of women. Let men walk in our shoes for once, then they'll see what our lives are like.' Ask Gioconda to record a video for me. I'd really love to have one."

I don't admit to her that one of the reasons I asked Gioconda for an interview is so I can tell her the effect she's had on Belén. I have a copy of her latest book, *Las fiebres de la memoria* (The Fevers of Memory), and I'm going to ask her to sign it for Belén.

I wait for Gioconda Belli at the press office of the Buenos Aires International Book Fair. She arrives with her publisher's publicity team. She looks exhausted. As one of that year's guests of honor at the book fair, she's been in and out of interviews since she got here. She's leaving tonight. But she doesn't bat an eye before recording a message.

Hi Belén,

I'm told you found my book Republic of Women *helpful while you were unjustly incarcerated. I want you to know that I was incredibly moved when I heard this, and it makes me so happy to know that my book helped you through such a difficult time, even just a little. Please don't lose hope, or strength. Remember you have a whole life ahead of you. Be happy, find joy, forget everything you've been through, or let it give you strength, because after darkness comes sunshine. Think of the sun.*

I hand her the book, and she signs it. I send Belén the video on WhatsApp. In response, I get a voice memo that just says, "Ay," followed by a long sigh.

46

WITHOUT FREEDOM WE ARE NOTHING

It's cold and windy in late July 2016 in Punta del Este, Uruguay. The actress Dolores Fonzi is getting ready to attend the Premios Platino del Cine Iberoamericano ceremony. She's been nominated as best actress for her role in *Paulina*, a movie by director Santiago Mitre in which she plays a lawyer who goes home to Misiones to collaborate on a social inclusion program. Despite being gang-raped, she carries on her work in the poor neighborhood where the incident took place.

She has a rolled-up piece of paper in her wallet. "Just in case," says her partner, Santiago, the movie's director. In the dressing room, she unrolls the piece of paper and writes FREEDOM FOR BELÉN.

The Punta del Este Convention Center is teeming with people from both the Latin American and Spanish movie worlds.

In the running for Best Actress are Antonia Zegers from Chile, Dolores Fonzi from Argentina, and Inma Cuesta, Elena Anaya, and Penélope Cruz from Spain. The host announces that the winner is Dolores Fonzi.

Before she hugs the people sitting with her, the camera shows Dolores taking out a piece of paper and then walking to the stage. TNT is broadcasting the event live in several countries, including Argentina.

"I want to dedicate this prize to all the women who have experienced violence or discrimination," Fonzi says onstage. "The state must stop infringing on our rights. Freedom for Belén. We are all Belén and, without freedom, we are nothing," she concludes and then holds up a sign with the words #FREEDOMFORBELÉN.

The image immediately goes viral. If there is anyone who still doesn't know Belén was in prison, this is when they find out.

"I'd love to meet the actresses who helped me. I adore them. Especially Griselda Siciliani, Dolores Fonzi, and Carla Peterson. One day I'd like to personally thank them for what they did for me," Belén says over a hamburger lunch in Constitución. In the stall, as in prison, when it's cold, it is very cold, and when it's hot, it is very hot.

47

TEN FRIENDS

"What are *amici* for? You've seen how it goes. Familiarity breeds contempt. We needed outside voices and support. The worst we can do is give the impression of being on our own. That's why some organizations offered to file an amicus brief, which worked well for us," Soledad tells me.

Amicus is Latin for "friend." In the glossary of difficult legal jargon, *amicus curiae* is a Latin expression that refers to briefs filed by a person or group that is not a party to the legal case but volunteers insight or expertise on some question of law or related matter in order to assist the court on the subject of the trial. Hence the name "friend of the court": *amicus curiae.*

Human rights organizations agree to file amicus briefs for Belén's case. Once more, they will exercise social and legal pressure by doing so in person, all on the same day. They will speak on record and at a press conference.

Amnesty Argentina's Paola García Rey and Mariela Belski are there again.

Celeste Braga Beatove, director of the Innocence Project in Argentina, is also on her way.

Ever since she first heard about the Belén case, Celeste has wanted to help. The second she found out about the call for amicus curiae briefs, she raised the issue with the heads of her organization. The

men had their doubts. A timely meeting with a group of feminist lawyers swayed them.

Now they will have to convince the Tucumán judges. One thing is
certain: they will need to argue in the realm of fact, not theory. There
will be time for that later. And the main fact in Belén's case is that
there was never any real evidence against her.

There was no DNA evidence. The report mentioned more than
one fetus, and none of them were preserved. The report claims a fetus
had been found at three in the morning. There are records showing
Belén was admitted at 3:50 a.m. There is no evidence, there simply
is none.

Raquel Asensio leads the Commission on Gender in the Public Defender's Office. The office does not intervene in local cases, especially
when a private trial lawyer is already involved, but was compelled to
join the brief. "It felt strategic to us as a violation of women's human
rights. The fact that the lawyer representing Belén, a well-known
feminist, was working pro bono played a part in our decision."

Raquel goes to the offices of Public Defender Stella Maris Martínez,
which are on the sixth floor of Avenida Callao 800. The two of them
had worked together before on what would become known as the FAL
case, in which the Supreme Court ruled that terminating a pregnancy
resulting from rape could not be punishable by law. "We have to join
the brief," they said at the same time. The idea was to examine what
bearing Belén's defense had on the conviction before Soledad started
representing her. It was striking how the public defender's role in the
criminal proceedings had been used in the conviction. "We'd never
seen anything like it. It just goes to show that the court had no interest
in giving her a fair trial."

There was a clear burden of responsibility on the court, which had
seen Belén's right to representation being steamrolled and taken no
concrete measures—like appointing new counsel or declaring a mis-

trial, or anything else that would ensure Belén's right to representation in the trial—and instead used that shortcoming to convict her.

What Raquel doesn't know, and almost nobody knows, is that Norma Bulacio, the public defender who was such a determining factor in Belén's conviction, had been to see one of the members of the Supreme Court of Tucumán while the case was being deliberated. She did this in secret, and I heard it from a judge. She told them her former client was guilty.

The arguments elaborated in the Commission on Gender in the Public Defender's Office were lifted almost verbatim from the opinion of one of the judges who later exonerated Belén. The majority opinion cited the Innocence Project brief, which Celeste had spent sleepless nights putting together.

In the end, a total of ten "friends" joined the brief.

When Edurne Cárdenas, a lawyer from Tucumán and member of the Center for Legal and Social Studies, bought her ticket home to visit her family six months earlier, she never imagined she would also be petitioning the Supreme Court of Tucumán to release a woman who was in prison for a miscarriage.

The other amici were the nonprofit Human Rights and Social Studies Lawyers in the Argentine Northeast (ANDHES), the Permanent Assembly for Human Rights (APDH), and the Criminal Thought Association (APP).

Later amici would include the Latin American and Caribbean Committee for the Defense of Women's Rights (CLADEM), the Latin American Group for Justice and Gender (ELA), and representative Soledad Sosa (of Workers' Left Front).

Nelly Minyersky, known as Pila, one of the pioneers of the National Campaign for Abortion, was there representing the Buenos Aires bar association. In the organizations' press conference, she said that "to read this file is to read impunity."

It was her eighty-seventh birthday.

On August 1, 2016, *Página 12* would run an interview with Belén on the front page. The headline read, "I Didn't Kill Anyone," in huge letters. The interview was conducted by one of the paper's regular journalists, Mariana Carbajal.

"She's been writing her story in prison. Her goal is to have it published in book form, under the pseudonym Belén. 'So that people will realize I'm just an ordinary woman, not a murderer, not the monster I've been made out to be.' The first thing she plans to do the day she's allowed to go home is take a cold shower with all her clothes on and then lie in bed hugging her parents, drift off, and sleep 'until my eyes hurt.'"

48

PILA

Nelly Minyersky goes by "Pila," though it isn't because her battery never runs out. When she was a little girl, her mom used to cut her hair a lot so it would curl. That's where "Pila" came from, because sometimes she looked bald, which is what the word means in Argentina. She was born in Tucumán, and even though she only lived there until she was seven, she feels like a Tucumana and a participant in the struggle to reverse the fact that her home province is one of the most backward in the country for the protection of women's rights.

She recently turned ninety, and we had lunch together in the Centro Cultural de la Cooperación, which is next door to her legal practice. "What happened in Tucumán is unbelievable. To think the province was an intellectual hub just decades ago. But everyone left. First because the factories closed, then because of repression."

She talks at length about her father, a Jewish immigrant who was driven out of Russia and into Argentina by poverty. He eventually settled in Tucumán. "He was always telling us that he would never forget how it felt to be hungry. He died young, at sixty-six. Before dying, he held my hand and made me promise that none of his descendants would go hungry. My mom was born in Buenos Aires and then lived in Tucumán. That's where they met. Dad's business was across the street from the house. My family was always talking about how angry my dad got when he had another daughter. But then, when my brother was born, I remember him shouting to our neighbor, 'Doña Rebeca, it's a boy!' I was four. And I remember the joy, the celebration."

Nelly graduated from the University of Buenos Aires in 1961 and began teaching there soon after. But following the police repression of La Noche de los Bastones Largos (the Night of the Long Batons) in July 1966, she walked out of the university in solidarity with the students and teachers who were beaten. She went back in 1973 and was forced out again during the civil-military dictatorship. She returned to her position with the reinstatement of democracy in 1983. To this day she teaches at the Faculty of Law, where she directs an interdisciplinary graduate program in social policies for children and young people.

Nelly mentions Soledad Deza regularly throughout the conversation. It's clear she admires Soledad as much as Soledad does her. "What she did for Belén is incredible." When Soledad decided to file an extraordinary appeal with the Supreme Court for the María Magdalena case, she asked Nelly for help because she wasn't licensed to practice law in Buenos Aires. The signature of Nelly "Pila" Minyersky is the one on the appeal.

"We've worked together on so many different projects since we met," Soledad reminisces. "She's also a loyal drinking companion!" Soledad laughs. Soledad is always laughing. She asks me what Nelly thought about the book idea.

She doesn't give me a chance to answer before saying, "She was the first person who said we needed to make a movie. I swear. It was back in 2016. She said Julieta Ortega or Natalia Oreiro should make a film about me. Hahaha. She didn't tell you!?"

Nelly and Soledad share a profession, a feminist vocation, panel discussions on gender and law, trips to the National Women's Conference, and an enviable sense of humor. In the photographs they each show me separately, they're both wearing bandanas. The two women were born in Tucumán; one still lives in the city while the other lives in Barrio Norte, Buenos Aires. Although several years separate them, they are united in their activism and their love of beer. Now, when they raise a glass together, they say, "Let it be law."

49

PATIENT FIRST, PRISONER SECOND

I have always thought that train stations stir our memories. You can't see the platform from Belén's stall, only the station's facade and other clothing stalls cluttered with socks, hats, sweatshirts of knockoff American brands, and a bit further on, Senegalese street vendors.

Sitting there, Belén begins to reminisce:

I don't know if I was walking fast because I was excited my case was finally being handled, but one day I went and twisted my ankle. I had to be examined at Hospital Padilla. It was sheer luck that they didn't take me to Avellaneda. Though one time I did go to the men's prison across the street, because that's where the dentists see you if there's something wrong. But the physicians at Hospital Padilla didn't treat me well, either. I was seen by an orthopedic surgeon, who was rude to me during the examination. He didn't want to create a medical record for me, claiming he needed a court order. But I told him I couldn't go back to prison and grit my teeth through the pain while I waited for him to get one. At the penitentiary, if you're in pain, they take you to the hospital. He said, "I'm used to dealing with prisoners" and I replied, "In here, I'm a patient, not a prisoner." It was Soledad who taught me about these things.

Ever since her case went public, whenever Belén leaves the prison for a doctor's appointment, she hears someone talking about her case. While she's waiting, she hears her case being discussed on TV. An older woman sitting next to her strikes up a conversation. "I can't believe what happened to that girl. It's so unfair. I can't believe they let something like that happen."

"You're right, ma'am, you're absolutely right," Belén replies without taking her eyes off the screen.

The woman tells her she still hasn't seen her face.

"Well, she doesn't go out, she doesn't talk to a lot of people," Belén replies with the confidence of a woman speaking about herself. Belén wants her to say more about what she thinks about her case. "What do you think about the judges who convicted her?"

"I don't know, I think they should be removed from office. They were certainly up to something."

"And the doctors?"

"You couldn't pay me to be treated by them or take my daughters to see them. I can't believe they're still allowed to be doctors, like nothing happened."

When Belén tells me this I say it must have been nice to hear that people were convinced of her innocence.

"Oh, there were plenty of people who never believed me."

50

A VERY SENSITIVE ISSUE

On July 30, 2016, Enrique Peña Nieto, then president of Mexico, travels to Argentina. Unsurprisingly, his visit will also include a meeting with President Mauricio Macri. Cecilia González, an Argentina-based journalist from Mexico and a correspondent for the news agency Notimex, requests and is granted an interview with the Argentine president.

Cecilia has been following the movement to free Belén for a while now, both on social media and in the few articles published about it. Until then, no journalist had had the opportunity to raise the issue with Macri. Cecilia decides to slip a question about Belén into her interview with the president.

Cecilia published the interview in her book, *Al gran pueblo argentino* (To the Argentine People):

Since your campaign, you've insisted that Argentina is in the twenty-first century. But there's still a twentieth-century issue that needs addressing, and that issue is abortion. There is a particularly high-profile case that mobilized organizations internationally: the Belén case, about a woman who was arrested and held in prison for two years after suffering a miscarriage. Doesn't a case like hers make you feel abortion ought to be legalized?

It's a very sensitive issue. Sometimes individual cases like these make you stop and think, but I would reiterate that what needs to be protected here is life.

What about the lives of women who die from botched abortions?

Yes. [The president is silent for a while] . . . Clearly, life needs to be protected. Bringing a child into the world is one of the most beautiful things a couple can experience. A person is the most beautiful expression of love in this world. I will always be on the side of life, regardless of any of the protocols that must be met. But I really do believe this is a core value in all our lives.

So, what you're saying is there's no chance of abortion being decriminalized while you're in office.

"Exactly," the president replied.

51

SISTERS FIGHTING

It's my final trip to Tucumán before finishing the book. Belén hands me a small but heavy bag to give to her sister Julia. I'm excited to meet her. The first few times I visited the city, I had this fantasy of tracking down my dad's family, whom I haven't heard from in twenty years, if not more. It isn't easy, because Correa is a fairly common surname in Tucumán. Eventually, I set aside the idea, although I don't abandon it completely. Either I'd meet them, or I wouldn't. For now, I'm just eager to see Belén's family. It all gets mixed up in my head. My dad hurt my mom a great deal; now they're both gone, and once again, much as it was when I used to always take my mom's side as a kid, something compels me to want to spend time around a woman who was injured by the patriarchy. I feel stronger now than when I was a little girl.

In the weeks running up to my trip, Soledad's colleague Luli campaigns to get Belén her high school diploma. The document shows the two incompletes, social work and public opinion, from her first case of peritonitis.

Julia and I text each other, and we meet at the Hotel Garden café, across from Plaza Independencia. She looks like Belén, except bigger, with the same enormous smile. Belén disagrees; her sister is blonder, with prettier eyes. "I'm the dark one, haha," she says in a voice memo on WhatsApp. Julia gives me a long hug and then shows me a faded Topper shoebox with some of the belongings Belén had asked her to bring. A few letters, a couple of books, and her high school notebook.

"I've been doing paperwork all morning. Turns out I wasn't getting my allocation per child, so I went to figure out why. They had my baby down as 'foreign,'" she tells me.

I can't believe what I'm hearing. Do these things only happen in Tucumán?

"No one in my family has ever left Tucumán. My baby is eleven months old but ANSES [Argentina's national social security administration] has him registered as foreign-born. We traveled abroad not long ago, and I wouldn't be surprised if that's why they got my son's information wrong."

I ask her to stay a while, but she tells me she has to get to work and that she left her son with her mother.

"Please tell me how Belén's doing. We're so grateful to the lawyer [Soledad]. Last week I ran out of money to buy diapers because I finally finished paying off the loan I took out for my sister's first attorney last month. You didn't know? We took out several loans. Luckily, one of them is settled. If it wasn't for Soledad and the angels who work with her taking on Belén's case pro bono, she would only be getting released from prison around now, and just for day trips. Instead, she's been free for three years," Julia says, smiling.

She's in a rush and doesn't want to sit down. Yet, she keeps talking.

"You have no idea how much we used to fight. Even though I'm younger than her, it's like I'm the older sister. We fight all the time. One time, in prison, I got so mad I left halfway through my visit. Then I didn't visit for three sessions in a row. You know why we fought when she was locked up? I think it was to make believe she was free and act like we did when we were kids.

"Luckily, the prison guards were always really nice to us. They never made us strip down at inspection. They'd tell me, 'With what you're wearing, there's nowhere to hide anything.'

"I used to be against it [abortion], but then I read a ton about the issue. Women have abortions for so many reasons. Now I know I have to be in favor of it. Everyone in my family changed their minds. I'm at every single march because I don't want anyone else to be sent to prison like my sister.

"I want Belén to be OK. I'm OK. I coach hockey, but it's not enough to support me and my son, so I went back to high school, and now I'm training to be a corrections officer. I liked how they treated us, so I thought I would be good at it. All right, then, I should get going.

"Thanks," she says and then leaves.

52

PIRINCHO

"You have to talk to Pirincho," I hear from more than one woman I interview. Pirincho is the nickname of Edmundo Jiménez, the chief prosecutor of Tucumán. But I can't get him to talk to me. Hewing to the tenet that judges speak through their judgments, Jiménez replies that he already issued an opinion. I insist. This was around the time Adriana Giannoni, a prosecutor who works in Jiménez's office, attempted to stop an eleven-year-old rape victim—known by the pseudonym Lucía—from getting an abortion and then prosecuted the two physicians involved in the legal termination of the pregnancy.

We can't know what happened between the moment the Belén case was ruled on and now, with Lucía's case, but Pirincho Jiménez's July 26, 2016, opinion was the light that began to illuminate the ghost train Belén was riding.

Jiménez claimed there was an initial defect in the illegitimate procedure that was carried out at the hospital, during which several of Belén's rights were violated: due legal process, right to counsel, the right against self-incrimination, the right to equal treatment, and the right to privacy.

As soon as Jiménez's opinion became known, the Tucumán newspaper *La Gaceta* changed its approach to the topic.

Jiménez considered Belén to have been "physically and psychologically" vulnerable, something that, in his opinion, the judges did not take into consideration.

"Belén did not know she was pregnant, nor did she look pregnant, according to testimonies from the people who saw her. [She] claimed that she never stopped menstruating and felt no movement in her belly, that her body was normal and her breasts hadn't grown. She and her mother, who also didn't realize she was pregnant, went to the emergency room for abdominal pain," he said.

With regard to her vulnerability, Jiménez noted that "it isn't enough for states to simply abstain from violating a person's rights. They need to take positive measures and offer special protections." In other words, in Jiménez's view, Belén received no support from the doctors and nurses who treated her.

He also echoed a psychiatrist's testimony in court, which aligns with the beliefs of many of us who read the case file and visited the hospital. "A person who wants to commit homicide—a person who knows they're going to have a baby and is determined to cause their death—simply doesn't go to a hospital."

53

SOLD-OUT MASKS

Days pass without news about Belén's case. The Provincial Organization to Free Belén calls a meeting. With Chief Prosecutor Jiménez's opinion and the United Nations pressuring the government of Argentina to do whatever mediation is necessary to get Belén released from prison, the organization feels it has to act quickly for the court to expedite her freedom.

"Let's call for a nationwide demonstration," Soledad says.

"Nationwide? But we're marching in Tucumán," says one of the organization members. "Well, we can put out a call for a demonstration in Tucumán but call it nationwide. Let's see what happens. Not every demonstration has to start in the capital." They laugh.

They call a press conference to announce a "large," nationwide march for August 12.

Celina writes to Mariana Cardello, the graphic designer who reached out to them from Mendoza. "Are you sure?" Soledad asked. "Because we can use all the help we can get, hahaha."

They ask her to design a flyer for the march. They post it on Facebook:

The Organization to #FreeBelén in #Tucumán calls for a NATIONWIDE MARCH this August 12. The demand for Belén's freedom and the overturning of her conviction needs

to be heard IN EVERY PUBLIC SQUARE ACROSS THE
COUNTRY.
#FreedomForBelén #ExonerateBelén

The digital poster for the protest call is shared over a thousand times in just a few hours. Requests for flyers come from cities and provinces across the country. Days later, universities and unions will join the movement.

The Workers' Party (PO) creates two videos of artists, journalists, and politicians making the same demand, among them the comedian Malena Pichot, the television presenter Úrsula Vargues, the actress Soledad Villamil, and the Chilean musician Ana Tijoux. "I'm here to send solidarity to our compañera Belén, who's been in prison for two years, and to demand her conviction be overturned. Fighters unite. My body, my choice." Joining them are also the journalist Silvia Martínez Cassina from Channel 13, and Soledad Sosa and Jorge Altamira from the Workers' Party.

The daily *Clarín* covers the video. It's the first time the newspaper is giving this much space to Belén. People on the Freedom for Belén Facebook page celebrate the fact that they made it into *Clarín*. But an even bigger surprise and victory is that Tucumán's very own *La Gaceta* is running news about the demonstration, which is now set to be held all over the country. "*La Gaceta* is talking about our march!!! We did it!"

Yanina Muñoz and Milsa Barros, from the Mumalá group, once again suggest wearing masks. They've already seen that the masks have power and send the right message. "It doesn't matter what Belén looks like, because what happened to her can happen to you, to me, to anyone." The Organization to Free Belén is excited about the idea, and Yanina and the Mumalá women start making arrangements.

They go to all the party supply stores in the center of San Miguel de Tucumán. The masks sell out, so they text their compañeras and ask them to check neighboring towns. They snap up every white mask. When in doubt, they also buy green ones. No one wants to miss out.

Unlike with a "green wave" and coordinated efforts from the "sisterhood" of representatives—the name given to the group of legislators from across the political spectrum who led the abortion debate in Congress—not a single major political party added its voice to the call for Belén's freedom. This is how representatives from the Workers' Party, the Left, and women from the Freemen of the South Movement, and Mumalá end up spearheading this grassroots movement.

On August 12, representatives from the Organization to Free Belén lead the march. Not far behind them are Belén's mother and sisters, who wish to keep their identities secret.

As they're arriving at the meeting point, Lucía, one of the women marching in a mask with PVC pipes made to look like prison bars, calls out to Yanina:

"I'm crying. I feel like I really, truly am Belén. All because of what's happening."

Soledad Deza reads a message from Belén through a megaphone:

In our society, when people want to hide something, they find someone to blame. They point their fingers at those who can't defend themselves, and they accuse them. They don't listen to them. These people become guilty because of their faces, their clothes, because they're poor, or because they're women like me.

The nationwide Freedom for Belén march is the largest of its kind in the province: three thousand women march together to the Tucumán courthouse. Women applaud and toss confetti from their balconies.

People in more than a hundred locations across the country spill into the streets to demand Belén's immediate release. In larger cities, the marches are even more impressive.

Around noon in Buenos Aires, the marchers stop in front of the courthouse. Just as in Tucumán, this is the place they choose to demand an end to a misogynistic justice system. By evening, everyone is there—the organizations from before, the activists from now, girls who are just finding out that women are being sent to prison for abortions. Everyone is surprised to see just how many women are showing up as well as their reasons for being there. International media also makes an appearance. At the front of the crowd are Marta Alanis, an educator and activist; Nelly Minyersky; Jenny Durán from Catholics for Choice; Victoria Tesoriero, a sociologist; Araceli Ferreyra and Myriam Breman, politicians; and Nora Cortiñas from the Mothers of the Plaza de Mayo. All are wearing green bandanas. "There are so many of us," some women say to each other.

Meanwhile, on Channel 8 in Tucumán, Fabián Fradejas and Dante Ibáñez, the judges who convicted Belén, still stand behind their guilty verdict.

54

SWING VOTE

Judge Daniel Posse from the Supreme Court of Tucumán will write the majority opinion in the Belén case. His profile is unusual for Tucumán Province, at least in the context of all that we've witnessed in the judiciary until now. He was secretary of human rights under Tucumán governor José Alperovich and has worked as a professor at the Faculty of Law for several years. In the human rights module he teaches every term, he screens a movie called *Swing Vote* starring Andy Garcia.

Swing Vote is set in an alternate reality in which *Roe v. Wade* has been overturned, leaving each state to determine its own abortion laws. In Alabama, abortions are illegal and punishable by death. Enter Virginia Mapes, a young Alabama lawyer. After getting pregnant by accident with a casual boyfriend, she decides she is unprepared to carry the pregnancy to term or raise a child, so she has a termination at a private clinic. Under the new Alabama abortion statute, she is charged with first-degree murder. This is how her case reaches the US Supreme Court. In this instance, the justices have to decide if Alabama's abortion law violates "the due process clause" and the right to privacy as enshrined in the Fourteenth Amendment. The movie illustrates the pressures on Justice Joseph Kirkland (Andy Garcia), who was appointed to the Supreme Court shortly before the court would have to rule on the case. These pressures enter the private sphere.

It's interesting to witness each justice's arguments and beliefs, from the man who believes wholeheartedly that Virginia Mapes should be imprisoned, to the woman who shares her own abortion story. With apologies for any spoilers, the justice played by Andy Garcia voices a memorable opinion, and Virginia Mapes's conviction is overturned. Daniel Posse uses this movie to illustrate the legal foundation for women's right to abortion and also to help his students understand what is known as the FAL decision, which cemented the rights of Argentine women who have been raped to seek abortions without criminal liability or court authorization.

Those familiar with Judge Posse, be it through his previous work in human rights or the content of his syllabus, could have predicted he would be against penalizing abortion. Posse, on the other hand, had the feeling that, for the first time in his career, he might have to play Kirkland's role in the movie: engaging in difficult conversations and facing enormous pressure in his academic, jurisprudential, and emotional lives. Maybe he thought he would have to argue about abortion rights with some of his colleagues before even reading the case file.

But none of this happens. When the brief reaches the Supreme Court, Posse's law clerk, Luis Acosta, is waiting. He has already highlighted a few sections. Posse doesn't even have the chance to sit down. He can't believe his eyes. He isn't going to have to convince anyone. No judge is going to uphold a conviction for a crime that was never proved. The file mentions two separate fetuses, one male and one female, and two different locations for where they were found. The timeline doesn't match Belén's movements. There is no DNA.

The first thing they have to rule on is Belén's pretrial detention. As there is no firm conviction—the ruling she was convicted under was instantly appealed—Belén should be free. It doesn't make sense for her to remain in prison. She doesn't pose a flight risk or any danger to others.

Insofar as the merits of the case are concerned, there will be time for them to present their argument.

55

WHAT'S THE MATTER, MOM?

In the 880 days she's been in prison, she's become used to almost everything. Everything, that is, but her mother crying.

"Why are you crying now, Mom? Mom, answer me. What's the matter?"

The warden gestures at her to end the call. The phone is in her office, and she's left Belén alone for a while to talk to her mother. "I told you to hang up," the warden insists.

Belén gets upset and says she won't do it. The prison staff has gotten used to this new version of Belén, who has changed since she met Soledad and her case went public.

One of the prison guards drags her by the arm to the main common area. "You don't get it, do you? Your mom is crying because she's watching the same thing we are."

"The Supreme Court has ordered Belén's release," says the news channel. Belén hears the words she has been dreaming of for months in the reporter's voice:

"The Supreme Court of Tucumán has granted one of Belén's lawyer's motions and ordered her immediate release while the appeal is ruled on. Belén was convicted of murder, but her lawyer insists her client had a miscarriage. Judges Daniel Posse, Antonio Estofán, and Antonio Gandur seem to agree with her. They have just ordered the sentencing judges of Chamber Three of the Criminal Courthouse to release her immediately."

Staring at the TV, Belén says, "Tell me I'm not dreaming." But no one can hear her for all the shouting and clapping. "You're getting out! You're getting out!"

She hugs her friends and then gets another phone call, this time from Soledad. "We did it. Didn't I tell you we could do it?" She cries.

Belén is flooded with memories. Her niece will finally get to see her as a free woman. Delfina is four now, and every time she visits Belén, she asks how long it will be until they let her out. She thinks of her father, whom she hasn't seen since the night of the hospital.

"I'm on my way," Soledad says.

Journalists begin arriving at the prison at the same time as Soledad. The prison staff know her well. Soledad doesn't want to say hello to anyone before Belén. She finds her, and their arms entwine until it's impossible to tell which of them belongs to whom. They dance.

"You're free, honey, you're free. Get your stuff together. We're leaving."

The prison warden grows serious and says they have to wait for her release orders before letting her out. Until then, she has to stay where she is.

"Are you kidding me! They want to make things hard every step of the way," Soledad says angrily. Then she tells Belén not to worry, just as she has since the first day they met. And Belén knows that Soledad always delivers. In the meantime, she starts thinking about how she will walk out of the penitentiary.

"Sole, I don't want anyone to see me. I don't want my face splashed on TV. I don't want people knowing what Belén looks like."

"No one is going to make you show your face if you don't want to. I promise."

The prison warden cuts in: "You need to walk out with your face uncovered. You have nothing to hide."

They'll leave that decision for later. For now, they need to expedite her release.

Soledad rushes downtown. When she arrives at Chamber III of the Criminal Courthouse, she is informed that they still haven't received the notice from the Supreme Court, and there's nothing they can do. At the Supreme Court, she is told that the notice is in process, and they will let her know when it is ready. It's late, it'll probably be ready by morning.

Hours pass and night falls again at the women's correctional facility. This is when Belén usually loses hope. Even though her release has been ordered, Belén will spend another night in prison.

56

AGAIN, THE WAIT

It's still dark out when they come get her. She doesn't have time to eat breakfast. Her sister Julia arrives early, followed by a patrol car. Belén is told she's being moved to the courthouse to receive notice of her release order. She asks if her lawyer has been informed, and they say yes, even though she hasn't. The journalists, on the other hand, have.

At the courthouse, they usher her into a small room, in handcuffs. Journalists from Buenos Aires and Tucumán are already crowding the old courthouse building.

At eight thirty a.m., Soledad Deza is being interviewed at a television studio. She is telling the host that they will push for exoneration. During the commercial break, Julia calls Soledad and says Belén is already at the courthouse. If she gets notice soon, they're going to escort her out in front of all the journalists posted at the door.

Soledad walks out of her TV interview and leaves the studio with Celina. They run the eight blocks to the courthouse.

"I can't believe I'm wearing heels on a day like this," Soledad scolds herself.

When she gets to the first floor, they don't want to let her into the room where Belén is waiting. "You're going to let me through because I'm her lawyer. You've done enough damage as it is. If you try to walk her out of here through the main door, you'll have to answer to the

Supreme Court," she says in the same firm tone she's used ever since she took Belén's case three months ago.

When they finally let her in, she finds her client in handcuffs. "I don't want anyone to see me like this, Soledad," she sobs. "I'm not a criminal."

The hubbub outside grows louder and louder. They're chanting. "The time is now! Free Belén! The justice system is to blame!" It's the women from the Provincial Organization to Free Belén.

"I know what to do," Soledad tells Belén and Celina. She pulls makeup out of her purse and starts applying it, using a lot of foundation to hide how red her cheeks are from running. "I'm going to talk to the press," she says.

Soledad walks downstairs and is instantly surrounded by journalists and microphones.

"Belén has been notified and is currently on her way back to the prison. Meanwhile, we'll be asking the court to expedite her release."

The press is thrown off her scent, and Belén goes on waiting in the courthouse. Five hours later, she finally sits in front of the clerk and receives official notice of the Supreme Court's decision: she is free. What Belén doesn't understand is why, if the decision has already been made, she has to return to prison.

"Are they going to torture me every step of the way?" she asks, crying. No one answers.

Soledad persuades them to take Belén out the back door. They drive her to the penitentiary, where she will continue waiting.

The Chamber III judges have ruled that Belén will need to pay a 40,000-peso bail for her to be released. The same judges who convicted her are now telling the press that the reason for the delay is that her family has yet to pay the issuance fee.

Belén is still in prison. Everyone knows her freedom is imminent, but Soledad isn't willing to have her client held in arbitrary detention for another minute, so she files a writ of habeas corpus with the

Supreme Court of Tucumán to expedite the process and then sits in the courthouse with two other members of the Organization to Free Belén.

The clerks of Chamber III, which put Belén away for almost three years, act as if the writ of habeas corpus doesn't exist and call Soledad to tell her that if she brings in the pending documentation the next day, they will order her client's release.

57

THIS MUST BE A DREAM

Word gets around that Belén will soon be released, and women's organizations march to the prison door. This time, on top of wearing white masks stamped with the words WE ARE BELÉN, they hold fuchsia balloons. The plan is to let them go the moment Belén sets foot on the street as a free woman.

Television production trucks set up outside.

Inside the correctional facility, Belén is also getting ready. She gathers her belongings—the letters she was sent, her books, her clothes. The books are heaviest of all.

Her friend and cellmate Vanessa offers to do her makeup. Belén accepts: "I want to look pretty for my mom, nephews, and nieces."

Vanessa applies liquid eyeliner, pink eye shadow, lipstick, and a lot of foundation. "You look like a movie star," the other inmates joke. Belén tries not to cry, so her makeup won't run.

Soledad, Celina, Noelia, and Luli, the four women who have been working on her case for the past four months, arrive at the penitentiary. The building is a din of laughter and shouting. The longer-term inmates and staff members can't recall another time like it.

Soledad tells her to hurry up: "Come on, let's get out of here. You're free." Belén hugs every last inmate.

Despite all that commotion, Belén still doesn't know how she wants to be seen leaving prison. The warden insists: "You need to understand that you're not a criminal. You have no reason to hide."

Soledad looks at Belén. "Do whatever makes you the most comfortable."

Belén thinks of her grandmother and her father. She doesn't want them to see her walking out of prison.

Luli cuts in: "I brought two masks just in case."

Belén likes the idea. She'll walk out with a mask on. Luli offers to wear the same mask. That way, no one will know which one of them is Belén.

She tries on the mask and realizes it spoils her makeup. "Ay, no . . ." she fusses. The women next to her laugh in response.

It's 8:18 p.m. on August 18, and the cellblock breaks into song and applause. The sounds travel over the wall and infect the women who have been waiting outside since morning.

"Let's go, I want to get out of here," she says all of a sudden.

The activists from the Organization to Free Belén form two lines to shield her from the cameras. Most of their masks are white, others green. But they are all the same: rigid, stern faces with two small eyeholes and the words WE ARE BELÉN.

The TV cameras snap the image they will use to illustrate their story: with a white mask over her face and a fuchsia wool hat over her hair, Belén walks the ten steps that separate the prison reception from the entry gate.

Belén steps onto the street. The first thing she sees are the fuchsia balloons, now floating up into the sky.

A few yards away, there are two cars. The women will split into both of them and drive in separate directions to lose the press.

The women who'd been waiting outside all day close in the moment they see her. Meanwhile, journalists try to interview the person they think is Belén.

With all the pushing and shoving, Belén falls on the ground. They help her up, then she, Noelia, and Celina go to the car. Celina's boy-friend is waiting in the driver's seat. The police officer at the entry gate holds Soledad back. "What now?" she asks. "Would you mind leaving me your card? I'm getting divorced and need some legal advice." Sole-dad takes out a pen and gives him her phone number. "Call me on Monday," she tells the guard.

"This must be a dream. This must be a dream. This must be a dream," Belén repeats.

After two years, four months, and twenty-three days in prison, Belén gets back some of her freedom.

THE MOON OVER TUCUMÁN

Several local media vans are tailing Belén and her "angels," which is how she refers to Noelia, Luli, and Celina. Apparently, a journalist is waiting at Belén's house. The reason for this is that the judges exposed Belén's real name in the release order, and *La Gaceta* published it. The women decide to take separate routes to throw the media off their scent. Aside from Soledad and the driver, no one removes their mask.

Belén's car pulls over outside their first stop: Soledad's house. They walk in and take off their masks. They can't stop laughing.

"Honey, do you remember the promise I made you?" Soledad asks Belén.

Belén recalls the most important promise anyone had ever made her and says: "Yes, you promised to get me out of prison."

"No, I promised we'd have a beer together one day," Soledad fires back.

After the hugs, laughter, and jokes, and once the tension finally melts away, they sit down. Soledad's husband, Marcos, passes them a couple of Norte beers, Belén's favorite. She's been dreaming of that flavor for close to three years. For a while, Belén, Soledad, Celina, Noelia, and Luli don't talk. They just drink.

Until finally Belén says: "Wait, I need you to come do something with me."

They all get up and go to the backyard, where they hold hands in a circle. The moon shines over Tucumán. "At the count of three, you're going to help me shout 'I'm free.' But really shout, OK?" she says, challenging them like she never has before.

"One."

"Two."

"Three."

"I'm free!" they yell again and again while holding each other.

59

FIRST WORDS

Her mother and sister arrive a while later, and the three of them go outside to shout Belén's freedom. That night, the two sisters don't fight.

Belén is nervous about seeing her father. But with all the journalists staked around her house, it will have to wait. "We're going to Grandma's," her sister says, practically an order.

Belén never let her grandma visit her in prison. "I was always the spoiled granddaughter, the most mischievous. I didn't want her to see me behind bars. She deserved better," Belén would tell me later.

When she walks into the house she so often dreamed of going back to, she hears her grandmother's voice: "Is that really her? Have they given me back my granddaughter?"

"Yes, Grandma. I'm back. They'll never keep us apart again," Belén says and runs over to hug her.

That night she sleeps in her grandmother's bed, just as she had when she was a little girl.

The next morning, her brother Ariel comes to visit. "He worked in Salta and was waiting to hear when they were letting me out. His boss is a good man and told him, 'Go on, go be with your sister, you should be there to welcome her home,'" Belén recalls now.

"I can't believe they're keeping you from going back to your own home. I'm going to take you there," her brother says. They set off to the house where her father, mother, and the rest of her siblings are waiting.

Belén spent a lot of time in prison thinking about what she would say to her father when she saw him.

She arrives at the house, and he opens the door.

The silence seems to last forever. Belén doesn't know what he's going to say.

"I made your favorite empanada" are the first words out of his mouth.

60

ARE YOU LOOKING FOR BELÉN? I'M BELÉN

While the Supreme Court was issuing its decision to end Belén's pretrial detention, the court that convicted her was releasing documents containing her real name. Even though Belén is still upset with most of Tucumán media, the truth is the majority of outlets chose to continue using her pseudonym despite having access to her given name. With the exception, that is, of *La Gaceta*. Soledad had to submit a writ of amparo to get the newspaper to stop publishing Belén's legal name.

But once was enough for the news of Belén's real identity to spread into the places she and her family frequent. Now that she is free, people begin seeking her out and asking about her.

Belén doesn't want to leave the house. She hears that people are asking about her around the neighborhood, at her old job, at her mother's and father's places of employment. She'd sooner stay locked up in the house. During her last few months in prison, she was allowed to choose who to see and who not to. Now people are coming to her neighborhood, to the places she goes to with her family. She is distressed beyond belief.

Soledad mentions this to the Organization to Free Belén. With help from Pan y Rosas—an Argentine women's group composed of members of the Workers' Left Front who actively participated in marches and other movements in Tucumán—they put together an online campaign to denounce the press's persecution of Belén and call for people to leave her alone.

The campaign consisted of people taking selfies with a sign that says ARE YOU LOOKING FOR BELÉN? I'M BELÉN. Men and women of all ages—some angry, others amused, some bearded, others very young—hold the same sign and post it online with a caption.

"They're trying to infringe on her privacy, to see her face. But what they don't realize is that Belén isn't just one person. She's thousands!"

Belén is all of us.

61

A NEW IMPRISONMENT

Pan y Rosas's quick thinking, plus the motion Soledad Deza and CLADEM filed for the judges to withhold Belén's real identity, seems to have had an effect. Journalists stop milling around Belén's house, although now and then strangers can be seen approaching the area, wanting to meet her. Belén doesn't feel she can begin any new relationships before readjusting to her old life.

The National Women's Conference in Rosario is happening soon, and it promises to be a good time: Belén is free, #NiUnaMenos has reenergized the women's movement, and Rosario is a city where women's rights are protected. Soledad tells Belén that a special working group will be formed to call for the Supreme Court to exonerate her. "I'd love to go," Belén says. She and the other women daydream about the trip they will take together.

Except she can't do it. She's been having panic attacks. The second she walks out of the house, she starts shaking and feels faint. Her heart races. She has regular fits of crying and rage. "It was like my body was still in prison, like it couldn't get used to me being free. Or my head," she tells me. Her mother thinks it's because she didn't eat well in prison.

The conference is starting the next day, and she sends a message to the WhatsApp group she has with Soledad, Celina, Noelia, and Luli: "I don't feel well. You all go and thank everyone for me." They don't try to convince her. "What if you record a message? That way they can hear your voice," they suggest.

She likes the idea. It's a way for her to be present.

She wants to start working again but doesn't know how she will manage if she can't even leave the house. One of the human rights organizations that advocated for her release offers to help her reenter the workforce. She asks them for a sewing machine. She can use the skills she learned in prison to make and sell plush toys. She doesn't have to go anywhere to do that.

Now, on top of calling for Belén to be exonerated, the Freedom for Belén Facebook page also posts the stuffed toys—a dog, a bear, a clown that looks like Piñón Fijo—and party favors she has for sale. Everything she learned to make in prison. As soon as she has a steady income, she wants to study literature.

"How did you get over the panic attacks?" I ask her.

"They told me to try therapy, but I couldn't make it to the offices, because I got dizzy every time I tried to leave the house. My family helped me with that—my mom, my sisters. They held me every step of the way and said, 'Don't be afraid, there's no rush, now take a firm step, good, you can do it.' And when I got frustrated, they would be there to tell me everything was going to be all right: 'You got out of prison, there's no way you can't get out of the house.'"

When Belén tells me this I can't help thinking of the panic attacks I had after my abortion. My three-year-old son and the babysitter would walk with me. The attacks continued into my next pregnancy and then as long as six months after my daughter was born. I worked through it with meditation and therapy. Thankfully, I had enough savings at the time to take a taxi to my appointments.

62

SOMETIMES WE FIND OUR WAY BACK TO OUR FIRST LOVE

In high school, Belén started dating. Jorge was from Paraguay but lived in Tucumán with his mom, who'd gotten a job there. Whenever the two half-jokingly, half-seriously argued—only to make up again later—he would say, "Just you wait, you'll end up marrying me one day."

Belén was devastated when Jorge said he was moving down to Buenos Aires after his mother found them better jobs in Lomas de Zamora. Jorge promised to come back for her, but she never believed him.

She wishes he could've been with her on their graduation trip to Tafí del Valle. It was beautiful, because Tafí is beautiful. The only thing missing was him.

Eight years passed. When Belén was sent to prison, Jorge heard about it from his high school friends. He immediately called Belén's house and spoke to her mother. He said he was living in Lomas de Zamora but could travel to Tucumán if Belén agreed to see him.

"I don't want him to come. I don't want him to see me here, in prison. Right now I need to focus on showing people how unfairly I was treated," Belén tells her mother. Her mind is made up.

Jorge called Belén's mom every month or so. "In case she changes her mind," he always said.

When Belén was finally released, he traveled to Tucumán and

didn't tell anyone. He'd heard that Belén had washed her hands of her ex-boyfriend, the one who'd gotten her pregnant. After he failed to visit her in the hospital even once, she sent him word that she never wanted to see his face again.

One afternoon, while Belén is home finishing the stuffed bear her neighbor commissioned for her daughter, she gets a WhatsApp from Jorge: "I'm in Tucumán. I'm coming to your house."

"You're really here? That's bold! Don't come to the house. Let's go get a drink," Belén replied.

Jorge says he never forgot her. That it made him sick to his stomach to find out what she went through. Belén felt something she'd forgotten in prison: the ability to love and trust another man.

"Come with me to Buenos Aires."

"I can't. I have to be with my family. I have to find a job."

"I'll get you a job there, then you can come live with me. We're going to get married, just like I said."

63

ANOTHER GUILTY
NEW YEAR'S EVE

Ever since the chief prosecutor filed a motion to have Belén's judgment vacated for reasons of manifest arbitrariness, her lawyers have tirelessly called for her immediate exoneration. As have the organizations involved. And there are more voices joining the cause every day. From the Women of Rosario Conference, from marches across the country held on November 25 for the Elimination of Violence Against Women. They're all calling for Belén to be exonerated. But the exoneration does not come.

Belén makes less than minimum wage selling plush toys. Soledad and some friends want to get her a job in the city government, but her criminal record keeps coming up. Celina asks Belén to clean her house from time to time, mostly as an excuse to help her out financially. With no money to spare either, she also has to take out a loan.

One day, Belén goes to the grocery store and hears a neighbor gossiping: "They released her, even though she's guilty. She definitely killed her baby."

On New Year's Eve, she raises a glass like she'd dreamed of doing during all the holidays she spent in prison, and she dances with her niece Delfina, who tells her, "Every night, I prayed for them to release you. That means I'm the one who got you out of prison." While shimmying around to a song by Ulises Bueno, Belén sends Jorge a message: "Find me a job. I want to be in Buenos Aires with you."

INTERNATIONAL WOMEN'S DAY

Jorge finds out that the factory where he works won't need more people until April. Meanwhile, he saves up money to buy Belén's ticket and a few items for the room they will share in the front of his mom's house.

Soledad waits for the judicial recess to end so she can go back to pushing for Belén's exoneration. "The Supreme Court's delay is unacceptable."

An international women's strike has been called for March 8, and organizations throughout Argentina are signing up, including members of the Organization to Free Belén and the brand-new #NiUnaMenos of Tucumán. They march and shout: "Ni una menos, vivas nos queremos." *Not one less, we women deserve to live.* There are new faces at every protest. Including Belén's. She is marching with her mother and her sister Julia. Together they hear someone shout into the microphone, "Exonerate Belén now!"

That's the day Belén meets Sebastián Pisarello, Celina's colleague at APA. Celina introduces them, and the two immediately get talking. They're almost the same age and height. It's like they've known each other all their lives.

When Belén leaves, Celina asks him how it felt to meet her.

"Who?" he asks.

"Belén. You just spent ages talking to her."

Neither of them knew who the other person was.

THE CITY OF RAGE

It's time to move to Buenos Aires. Belén doesn't have a job, the Supreme Court is dragging its heels, she still feels threatened by the press, and her old employer doesn't have a place for her anymore. Her family is not enough to console her, not even her beloved Delfina. And she doesn't want to be a burden. Waiting for her on the other side is a job and the possibility of reconnecting with the love she dreamed of in Tafí.

She gives most of her clothes to her sisters and friends but keeps the letters, the postcards, and the books. She puts them all in a box that she stores at her mother's.

The morning Belén sets out from the San Miguel bus terminal, her pack is light. With her again is her sister. True to character, they fight on their way out of the house. "If you don't hurry up, you're going to miss the bus," Julia yells while Belén frets over what else to take.

They get to the terminal with plenty of time to spare, so they sit down to drink a cup of mate. The terminal resembles a shopping mall, a very lovely one. There are designer stores, cute cafés, and two cinemas. Everything is nice and clean, and it doesn't have the same gloomy air as other bus terminals in the provinces, or the unease, deprivation, and abandonment that mark the terminal in Retiro, Buenos Aires.

It's twenty-three hours from San Miguel to Buenos Aires, the longest trip of her life.

"There was a lot of traffic that day, and it took forever to get into the city. Is it always like that?" she would ask me later.

Throughout the trip, she texts Jorge, who will be waiting for her at the terminal.

"It made me so happy to see him. I was crying over everything I was leaving behind, but I just needed to move on," she says, reminiscing about that moment.

They take the subway to Constitución. It's her first time riding a subway, and she doesn't enjoy it. Too many people crammed together. When they get to the train station, she manages to relax. "You'll get used to it," Jorge says. She doesn't think she could ever get used to all the shoving or the stress on people's faces.

She likes the Roca line, on the other hand, which goes from Constitución to Lomas de Zamora. "It's faster than the train to Tucumán." She laughs. The train from Retiro to Tucumán is famously slow: it takes twenty-three hours to cover the eight hundred miles that separate the capital from the northern province.

Jorge's mother and her partner are waiting for them at home.

"How are you? What have you been up to all these years?" she asks.

"Nothing much. Things in Tucumán are pretty quiet."

66

ARE YOU SITTING DOWN?

It's been two weeks since Belén moved to Buenos Aires, and she's already made friends with the neighbors. She's with one of them, Carla, and Carla's sister-in-law, Alicia, when her phone rings. Belén is surprised that Noelia would call without texting. She knows Soledad is traveling with her family; because of her case, she hadn't been on vacation in a year and a half. The truth is, Belén is terrified. Since her release, there's not a day she hasn't felt scared that she will be sent back to prison. Sometimes she wakes up at night screaming, "No, don't take me! I didn't do anything wrong." She knows that if Noelia is calling, then it's important.

"Are you with someone? Listen, go somewhere you can be alone and sit down," Noelia says. Belén had told them that the only person in Buenos Aires who knows the truth about her is Jorge. She's so nervous she says yes and then doesn't move.

"The Supreme Court just issued its decision. They exonerated you, honey. They're saying you're innocent."

She cries harder than she has since all of this started and feels truly free for the first time. She can finally leave behind the fear she's been carrying with her since the nurse showed her the cardboard box and called her a bitch. She can erase the word "homicide" from the report the police officer wrote when he came into her room right after her surgical procedure. Carla and Alicia express concern, but she says everything is fine and then shuts herself in the bathroom. She has no one to hug, because Jorge is at work. She looks in the mirror and utters the words she would like to say to the whole world: *Didn't I tell you I was innocent?*

67

PRISON OR DEATH

All the issues Soledad Deza raised were acknowledged in the Supreme Court's decision. First of all, the breach of professional confidentiality:

> *The doctor has a legal obligation to maintain confidentiality unless expressly told otherwise by the patient. The patient's silence can in no way be seen to provide a valid and rational motive to breach the physician's duty to professional confidentiality.*

All the evidence adduced in Belén's case was deemed inadmissible. The physicians' and midwives' testimonies were in themselves a crime. She was convicted without valid evidence.

The Supreme Court of Tucumán cites the plenary decision on the "Natividad Frías" case in the Federal Court of Appeals for Criminal and Correctional Cases, which at the time of Belén's conviction was already being cited in courts and law schools across Argentina going back thirty years. In that case, the court ruled that "women who have induced their own abortions or permitted others to do so cannot be arraigned on the basis of reports made by medical professionals, whether or not they were exercising their profession or official employment when they became aware of the fact."

In the case in question, a woman was prosecuted after hospital staff filed a report against her due to complications from an induced abortion. The sentence quotes an excerpt of Judge Lejarza's opinion, which helpfully summarizes the fundamental approach of that decision, this decision, and of the laws we hope will eventually be passed:

> *Article 18 of the National Constitution states that "no one can be compelled to testify against himself." It is a cruel, latent, and ignoble violation of this precept to use the distress of a woman who had an abortion to report her crime, a crime that either came to light through a confession that was to all effects wrenched from her, or through a state of physical and spiritual helplessness that should not be exploited to those ends. . . . "Moreover, public interest cannot justify so inhuman a dilemma: prison or death."*

68

A SEALED ENVELOPE

On the right to privacy in the Belén case, the finding is reminiscent of the opinion of Judge Carmen Argibay, the first woman to be democratically appointed to the Supreme Court, in relation to a wholly different case. In this case, known as Baldivieso, a man goes to the emergency room in extreme physical distress only for capsules of cocaine to be found in his body during surgery. He was reported to the police on the basis of the evidence retrieved from his digestive system, but the Supreme Court would go on to rule that the body, like written correspondence, is inviolable.

In her opinion, Judge Argibay wrote:

> *Article 18 of the National Constitution specifically protects the residence, letters, and private papers—that is, spheres of an individual's private life—against arbitrary invasions, especially those perpetrated by agents of the state. . . .*
>
> *In this sense, it is difficult to conceive of a sphere more "private" than an individual's own body. In fact, if the constituents found significant reason to protect from government interference those personal matters contained "in an envelope" (the residence, letters, and private papers, as stated in the Constitution)—in other words, a sphere less proximal to the*

*person—then there is even more reason to find that this protec-
tion extends to the individual's very body.*

*In effect, the right of individuals to disallow third parties
from invading or interfering with their bodies is an essential
component of a private life, where personal autonomy is paramount, such that this sphere should at minimum share the same
expectations of privacy as the sites listed in the Constitution.*

At the end of the day, our body should not be more vulnerable and
violable than an envelope.

69

REMEMBER ME?

While regaining some of her composure, Belén calls Jorge and tells him she needs to go to Tucumán right away to be served official notice of the court's decision. She's had money set aside in a jar for just this moment. There's no time to say goodbye, and she immediately leaves for Retiro.

Noelia is waiting for Belén at the terminal and walks her to the courthouse—the one she went to as a woman accused, convicted, released, and now finally exonerated. It's a simple enough procedure. She just has to sign on the dotted line to be served official notice. Noelia needs to get back to the Fundación Mujeres x Mujeres, and Belén tells her she is going to stay a bit longer so she can read the verdict. The court employees chat with Belén and congratulate her.

As Judge Posse writes in his opinion:

The fact that law enforcement received incriminating information about Belén from the physicians treating her, a vulnerable woman in need of care[:] This is only the first instance of proof of the institutional violence *committed against the young woman, given that this breach of professional confidentiality was followed by a series of events that is inconsistent with the kind of treatment an individual in a clear state of vulnerability can expect to receive—in this case a woman who went to the hospital for urgent medical attention. She was incriminated as the perpetrator of a crime and accused from the very first moment of lying when she alleged that she knew nothing about her pregnancy; she was shown a box with the body of a dead baby boy as a form of moral punishment; she was subjected to a medical intervention without explanation as to the reason and scope of the procedure; her rights to confidentiality and privacy were violated in a blatant breach of the medical team's duty to maintain confidentiality, which went so far as to allow law enforcement to enter the space where a D&C was being performed. In other words, the accused was relegated from her status as patient and instantly treated as a culprit.*

That's what I've always said, Belén thinks and then continues reading.

Reading the verdict alerted me to a circumstance I have never once encountered in my long career as a lawyer and a judge: the ruling takes as one of the grounds for conviction the strategic posture of the court-appointed defense attorney.

I've had to intervene as an appeals judge in cases where the defense was poor and sometimes even nonexistent. However, I've never before encountered a case where the defense's actions, as described in the verdict of this case, were directly incriminating. . . . It is unheard of for numerous passages of a verdict to refer to statements made by the court-appointed defender in order to support the grounds for the conviction. If the public defender was seen to be incriminatory or acting against the interests of her defendant, the Court, far from endorsing this behavior by issuing a guilty verdict, should have removed the attorney in question and appointed another defender, or if that was not possible, dismissed the proceedings in light of the serious repercussions on the defendant's right to counsel and due process, which stemmed from a clear lack of effective court-appointed counsel. . . .

The sentence listed repeated instances of incompetent representation, which the Court deemed more useful in convicting the defendant than attaining her acquittal. Belén would have been better served with no defense counsel at all than with the category of defense described.

This is when Belén has the idea: *Everyone needs to know I'm innocent.* She asks the employee who's always been kindest to her to point her to the Criminal Court offices.

She goes to the office and asks to speak to the attorney in charge. She gives her real name. Norma Bulacio looks across the desk at Belén but doesn't recognize her.

Belén stands in front of Norma Bulacio and tells her what she has dreamed of saying for so long: "Do you remember me? You told me to plead guilty. I promised I'd come see you when I was found not guilty. The ruling proved me right. You were a terrible lawyer."

And she leaves.

The next morning she returns to Buenos Aires, no longer scared of being sent back to prison.

A NEW LIFE NOT SO DIFFERENT FROM EVERYONE ELSE'S

Belén finally gets to celebrate her exoneration in Buenos Aires with Jorge. She wants to eat a hamburger at the train station before returning home. That night, they dance and hug, and he tells her the worst is behind them.

She begins working at the same factory as Jorge. They love having breakfast together early in the morning and then commuting to the factory in Burzaco. Things seem to be working out, and the two dream of going to university. He wants to be an engineer or a lawyer. She wants to study literature or social work.

But sales have decreased significantly in the last year. The factory needs to make cuts and lays off half its employees, including Belén, one of the most recent hires.

One of the women who was laid off hears about an opening for cleaners at the Constitución train station. She tells Belén, and the two of them go speak to the man in charge. He takes their information and calls Belén up the following month.

She has to wake up very early every day. She can't eat breakfast with Jorge anymore, though she does get home in time to make him lunch. She cooks empanadas once a week so that she misses home a bit less. She talks to her mother every day and sends Delfina voice memos. Soledad lets her know when anyone wants to talk to her, but Belén isn't usually interested.

She does speak to some people she knows have helped her cause. She needs a hand getting a better job. But whenever anyone says that her employment is contingent on revealing her real identity, she turns them down. Whenever she is offered work as a cleaner, she says yes. Her sister Julia asked me once if I'd realized how intelligent and capable Belén is. I told her I had. I know Belén realizes this, too.

The owner of the bar offers her a gig. Belén is capable of almost any kind of work, but she especially likes the idea of bartending. *Maybe they'll let me work in the kitchen one day*, she thinks.

A YEAR AFTER I WAS BORN AGAIN

One year after her release, a message is posted on the Freedom for Belén Facebook page.

Belén, a young Tucumán woman who was exonerated after eight years of arbitrary detention for a miscarriage, wants to be heard on the first anniversary of her freedom.

BY BELÉN

Two days from now will be the first anniversary of the date I effectively regained my freedom.

How will I ever forget the day I set foot on the street again! With my angels Sole, Luli, and Noe.

How will I ever forget how much they helped me!

How will I ever forget all the women who spent hours waiting to welcome me outside!

How will I forget my fellow inmates and the prison guards and the night we said goodbye!

How will I ever forget my family, who was anxiously waiting for me!

How will I ever forget that day! Everyone awaited my return after two and a half years of unjust imprisonment.

How will I ever forget that was the day . . . I WAS REBORN!

How will I ever forget the day one of my angels put a pencil to paper and wrote down the words I couldn't speak!

It was Celina De la Rosa from APA! She forced the media to give me a voice.

A year after my release I can only give thanks to God and my angels. Who is it that said we don't have angels? I can testify today that they exist. And you know what? I have four of them.

How will I ever forget that amid all the anxiety and distress, my angels were there with me, holding my hand and listening! I am eternally grateful.

THANK YOU!

Thanks to every woman and every organization, to the women's movement and to all the people who did their part to help me, who put on their "Freedom for Belén" T-shirts and went into the street to fight for my freedom.

BELÉN'S ANGELS

Who are the angels Belén references in her post?

To me, one of feminism's greatest triumphs is that women are no longer ashamed of crying. Gone is the image of the unprofessional woman who has to rush to the bathroom to cry because she doesn't want to be seen by her work colleagues.

Soledad, Celina, Noelia, and Luli have cried a great deal since they found out about what happened to Belén. And as they cried, they also started a small but important revolution.

Soledad Deza, the lawyer who found out by chance that Belén was in prison and would not rest until she was free and exonerated of all wrongdoing.

Celina De la Rosa, the journalist who from day one handled all communications for the case and also provided emotional support for Belén and her family.

Noelia Aisama, a lawyer, was twenty-six years old when she joined the team that worked to free Belén. For her, meeting Soledad was either an accident or destiny. Noelia had signed up for a lecture at the Faculty of Law about the responsibility of the state and instead accidentally walked into Soledad's lecture on the FAL decision.

I remember being blown away by what she said. The FAL decision touched me personally. In 2010, when I was studying in

*Buenos Aires, I miscarried. I was pregnant and have cardiopul-
monary issues. Until I met Soledad I had no idea I was eligible
for a legal termination. But since the FAL decision hadn't been
issued yet, getting a legal abortion was an ordeal. I miscarried
from all the uncertainty and the stress. You wouldn't imagine
how badly they treated me when I got to Hospital Argerich. I
didn't want to talk about the subject ever again, let alone think
about it. Until I met Sole.*

*I remember how anxious I felt hearing her discuss the FAL
decision. When the lecture ended, I had this urge to connect
with her. I didn't really know why at the time, but I looked her
up in the conference program so I could attend another one of
her lectures the next day. Again, I was filled with this need to
know more, except now I wanted to help, this time I knew what
I wanted to contact Sole so she could tell me where to find more
information, then use that information to make sure no other
woman went through what I had gone through.*

*I remember awkwardly going up to Sole and confessing my
secret in a few words. I said I'd miscarried and didn't know if it
was legal and could she tell me where to find more information
so I could help make sure no other women experienced what I
had experienced. She smiled and handed me her card. "Let's talk
next week." I wound up working at her practice, which is how I
became involved in Belén's case.*

In 2016, at twenty-four years old, lawyer Luciana Gramaglio is the
youngest of the group. They call her Luli, and she was born in Orán, a
city in the north of Salta Province, just a short distance from Bolivia.
She moved to San Miguel to study law when she was eighteen. The
only university in the capital of Salta is Catholic, and Luli wanted to
go to a public college. She'd attended religious schools from preschool
onward and was eager to try something new. Since she was a young

girl, she'd always wanted to help people, but she didn't know if she wanted to be a psychologist or a lawyer.

Luli and Noelia met in college, and Noelia introduced her to Soledad, whom she had been helping with research on obstetric violence.

One evening we all got together at Soledad's house. That's where I met her, and she told me about some of the obstetric violence and abortion projects she was working on.

A few days later, Soledad had to leave the city. She phoned me to say that María Magdalena had been called to the courthouse and could I go with her. María's doctors had tortured her and turned her in after she had a miscarriage.

From then on, we kept in touch, and a few months later she sent Noelia a note saying she was thinking of setting up a feminist law practice and were we interested in taking part. I didn't think twice before saying yes.

Soledad shared several experiences with Noelia and Luli. Like jumping through hoops to track down the case file or tacking up posters for the march with homemade glue at night. Like visiting Belén. Providing emotional support for her family. She also delegated press interviews to them when there was a sudden onslaught of media interest.

The day of Belén's release, Celina was tasked with coordinating press relations, among other things. She had help from her APA colleague Sebastián Pisarello, who would also be covering the event for their news agency.

That's when Luli and Sebastián met. Right before Luli went to meet Belén in prison with a pair of masks tucked into her handbag, she was interviewed by Sebastián.

I recently heard they've been together for two years.

I'm not sure how much of a motivating factor that event was. It feels like a family legacy: our social commitment and the pain we feel about injustice. Two bombs were set in my grandfather's law practice in 1975. Right after the coup, a police commissioner warned him that he was on a list of future desaparecidos. My grandfather decided to stay and fight to the end. That conviction lives inside me, inside everyone in the family—"Los Pisarello."

Today, Sebastián is one of the most engaged activists for the rights of women and girls in Tucumán. I thought this was worth mentioning.

Everyone involved in the Belén case feels like it has changed their life. At some point in the interview, they inevitably cry. But they are all—we are all—stronger.

THE PATRIARCHY THAT WILL NOT FALL

The owner of the bar where Belén works starts making comments about her looks and the clothes she wears. At first, she brushes them off. And then one day, he asks if she wants to go somewhere after work. She quits.

Since people at the train station know her, she asks the man in charge of the clothing stalls if he has any work, and he tells her there's a woman who needs assistance running her booth. She speaks to the woman and is offered the job on the spot. The hours are ten a.m. to eight p.m., Monday to Saturday. In the summer, it's Monday to Sunday. The pay is low, and the work under the table: no health insurance, social security contributions, or any other benefits. But at least she has a monthly salary. If things don't work out, she can always go back to working as a cleaner at the station. The factory has cut Jorge's hours so they won't have to lay him off. Belén doesn't hesitate before taking the job at the clothing stall.

That's where she is working the day I meet her.

MAYBE IT'S THE PASSAGE OF TIME

Belén and I always meet in the same places. At the clothing stall in the train station, at the burger joint, at my house, and in El Rosedal. But mostly we meet at the clothing stall, because she doesn't get a lot of time off. So we talk for hours on holidays and weekends. No one ever buys anything when I'm there. People stop and ask questions but never make the purchase. "I don't have enough money," they say, as if by apology. I bet some things sell during rush hour, but not much.

Close to two-thirds of the clothing stalls at the train station are staffed by women. The rest are staffed by men, most of them Senegalese. I assume no one there has legal work.

Belén is clearly well liked. The cleaners and women from the other stalls are constantly stopping by to say hi or tell her something. She introduces me to them as her friend.

The other day, I was checking the Freedom for Belén Facebook page and saw a picture of my aunt at one of the marches. She told me she'd never gone to any, so I called her: "I thought you said you never went to any marches? I found you, haha." Then she said she'd been to all of them but was too embarrassed to admit it to me.

The worst thing about prison? Whenever my niece Delfina left. I always wanted to leave with her.

I wouldn't live in Tucumán again. One TV channel broadcast a picture of a dead fetus next to my case file. Why would I want to go back after all that? But I would like to visit for New Year's and my mother's birthday. That's my dream. That, and going to Mar del Plata.

I never get that angry, really. But when I heard Senator Silvia Elías de Pérez saying there aren't any women in prison for abortions, I was so furious I started jumping and shouting. A senator from Tucumán, of all places! Is she going to pretend she never heard about my case? I'm still furious.

Senator Silvia Elías de Pérez was one of the most visible and vocal opponents of the bill to legalize abortion. The only day she missed a congressional session was the day Soledad Deza spoke about the Belén case.

Belén hasn't been to a hospital in three years. She still has nightmares of physicians and police officers storming into the operating room. She still feels scared because of how she was treated that night long ago. Yet she isn't a fearful person.

Only now do I ask her if she ever plans to go public.

"I guess one day I'll probably have to tell people I'm Belén. But I'm taking things slow for now."

"I have some news. We're getting married next year. Hopefully in Tucumán. You have to come," she says and then stops. A woman is asking about a blouse. She likes it but isn't sure about the price. She spends a while looking at the T-shirts.

"It feels really weird to be sitting here with you and talking about what happened without crying. Maybe it's the passage of time."

At one of our last meetings, at a McDonald's, she asks me to recommend a doctor. Of course, I say.

75

THREE YEARS LATER

There are some dates Belén will never forget. The date she went to the hospital, the date she was arrested, the date she met Soledad, the date of the national march to free Belén, the date she was released, and the date she was exonerated.

On August 12, it will be three years since the march. Belén and I discuss how we will celebrate the three-year anniversary of her release.

Every year on that day, her mom gives her a pair of white shoes like the ones she wore when she walked out of prison. But her mom won't be joining us this year.

Argentina's primaries are on August 11. Belén and I text, and she tells me there are a ton of people lined up to vote at her polling place, which is at a local school. She tells me not to wait too long before voting.

She says I remind her of her sister. Maybe it's because I'm absent-minded. In any event, I get up the courage to ask if she wants to write or say anything for the third anniversary of her release, thinking she'll write it later when she has some free time.

Instead, she sends me a WhatsApp seconds before it's her turn to vote.

It's been three years since I was released, and I feel enormously happy and grateful to everyone who helped me through the most difficult time

*of my life. Today, I am firm in my decisions. I'm not the weak woman
I was back then, broken by a patriarchy that, 6 years ago, sentenced
me to 8 years in prison for a crime I didn't commit. Now I am a strong
woman pumping her arms in the air and calling for an end to the unjust imprisonment of women for abortions. It's been three years since
I was released and I am here, yelling at the top of my lungs: we can do
it, girls, the patriarchy will fall!*

Sorry, I got carried away.

76

PUBLICATION

A few days later.

I tell Belén it's time for us to go sign our publishing contract. We make plans to meet at the entrance to the press's offices at noon. We're both coming from opposite directions, as on the day we met.

"Can I bring Jorge? It's a big day for me."

"Of course!"

We text each other to say we're running late and wind up getting to the corner of Avenida Independencia and Virrey Cevallos at the same time.

It's very cold. She's wearing lipstick and her eyes are glassy. We hug.

"You're wearing makeup. You look lovely."

"I'm just so excited. I feel the same as the day I set foot on the street, when I was released."

Julieta, the publicist, is waiting in the lobby. The book's editor, Rodolfo, joins us shortly after. I'm so nervous I forget to introduce Jorge, but luckily Rodolfo jumps in. Before heading upstairs, we stand in front of the new-releases display. Rodolfo tells Belén and Jorge to choose any book they like. Jorge doesn't bat an eye before selecting

The Lion King and *Ernie Pike*, a new edition of the comic series by the beloved author and journalist Héctor Oesterheld and Hugo Pratt. Belén says she needs to think.

I remember that one of Oesterheld's daughters, Diana, was kidnapped in Tucumán during the military dictatorship. She was six months' pregnant. Her husband, Raúl Araldi, was murdered. But I digress.

"There must be a place where these tragedies, made from courage and missed connections, can be written in favor of humankind. There must be . . ." said Héctor Oesterheld's cartoon character, Ernie Pike.

We head up to one of the publisher's offices. Belén is calmer now. Jorge wants to sit off to the side, a bit farther away. We all feel more at ease after a while and start cracking jokes. At some point, we begin talking over each other: the editor, the publishing staff, and me. Until finally Belén says: "I'd like to say something."

And then she explains why she hadn't spoken until then. She'd like to go to the launch event, though she doesn't know if she will in the end, since she still isn't ready to reveal her identity. She'd also like there to be a book event in Tucumán, with Soledad. She'd like her family and friends to be able to attend if they want.

"Wouldn't it be nice if someone sang?" I ask.

"Well, if you're going to start talking crazy, then I want Chayanne."

We laugh. We start speaking over each other again. The publishing staff call her Belén. I ask: "What name do you want them to call you?"

She answers: "My real name." Then she says it.

We take a picture of the two of us signing the contract: no faces, only our hands on the document, per Belén's request. Everyone leaves, and Rodolfo asks Belén if she knows what book she would like yet. "I prefer it when people choose books for me. When they try to guess which one I will like." So I recommend a thriller called *Errantes* by Florencia Etcheves.

When it's just the three of us, Belén asks Jorge to take another photo. This time, she wants our faces to be in the picture.

77

THE GREEN WAVE

In 2018, the debate to legalize abortion cascaded into the streets, the news, social media, and dinner-table conversations across Argentina.

The year kicked off with the actor Facundo Arana claiming that women are only fulfilled once they become mothers, and the actress Muriel Santa Ana replying that she'd had an abortion when she was twenty-four.

People called her a killer and wished cancer and death on her.

For #NiUnaMenos, there was no going back. The slogan spoke to so many women that more and more groups started popping up in the provinces, at universities, in organizations, within activist circles, each in its own fashion. We needed to ask for more.

On February 1 of that year, Jorge Rial, a famous television host in Argentina known for his misogyny, interviewed the journalist Luciana Peker, who told him that the country's televised media was turning its back on a groundswell being led by Argentina. "I think people are terrified of feminism." In response, Rial promised, on air and on social media, to make room for the abortion debate on his show, *Intrusos*. The next episode, he wore a green bandana. Then he invited the journalist Ingrid Beck, the author Florencia Freijo, and the comedians Malena Pichot and Virginia "Bimbo" Godoy, among others, to discuss the topic.

A protest was called on February 18, a "Green Action Day" for legal abortion. The turnout was unbelievable. There were so many people I started having panic attacks again. I believe attendance may have been even higher than at the #NiUnaMenos march in 2015. I'm almost certain. As soccer writers like to say, "the playing field was tilted."

On March 1, President Macri used the word "abortion" for the first time during the opening of the ordinary sessions of Congress. "We open this up for debate."

The wave persisted and grew. I remember attending a meeting at one of the National Campaign for Abortion headquarters. I'd gone there with Ingrid Beck and journalist Paula Rodríguez to bounce around some ideas about how we could reach an even wider audience. We talked about a thousand things, among them the possibility of encouraging journalists and authors to don the green bandana. One of the girls worried they wouldn't be able to restock the bandanas fast enough if they became too popular. Marta Alanis from Catholics for Choice replied, as insightful and even tempered as ever: "If everyone begins wearing green bandanas and street vendors start selling them, then we'll know our movement is a success."

The main campaign on International Women's Day was legalizing abortion. People in cities all over the country marched for that cause.

On April 26, the author Claudia Piñeiro gave the opening speech at the Buenos Aires International Book Fair. Dressed in green, she mentioned the campaign to legalize abortion. In reference to the author's role in society, she said that "four hundred writers agreed to defend the law for the voluntary termination of pregnancy with our signatures and our bodies." Then she reeled off a long list of books on the subject of abortion. She finished by holding the bandana in a closed fist above her head. Everyone in the room followed suit.

The Public Defender's Office put together a report on the number of criminal cases initiated for self-induced abortions between 2011 and 2016 in Argentina. The only provinces not to respond were Salta, San Juan, and Tucumán.

Many of the 690 speakers who appeared in the Chamber of Deputies during the monthslong debate to legalize abortion mentioned the Belén case. In fact, every one of the amicus curiae who spoke during the round of presentations made note of it. Meanwhile, the majority of people who spoke against legalizing abortion neglected to mention what had happened to Belén.

Soledad Deza was asked to present on the case. She explained that at that moment there were 534 lawsuits in Tucumán relating to abortions: "In ninety-seven percent of these, the women who had the abortions are the ones being arraigned," she illustrated. "The state not only prosecutes induced and self-induced abortions but also noncriminal abortions. Twenty-four percent of the lawsuits refer to adverse obstetric outcomes such as spontaneous abortions or miscarriages."

According to a piece Estefanía Pozzo published in *El Cronista* and based on data from the Senate Committee on General Legislation in the Chamber of Deputies, more women than men spoke before the representatives: 64 percent and 36 percent respectively.

The majority of women were in favor of legalizing abortion (60 percent) while a majority of men were against it (68.5 percent).

Four trans people took part in the debate, equal to 0.6 percent of the speakers. All were in favor of legalizing abortion.

One week before the representatives convened in the jury room to deliberate, I published a short crónica on the online platform *La Agenda* about my own abortion experience after being diagnosed with a nonviable fetus. I had never discussed it publicly.

The green wave reached its peak the day the bill was voted on in the Chamber of Deputies. After twenty-two hours of debate and a few last-minute vote shifts, at 10:02 a.m. on June 14, 2018, Argentina's lower house passed the bill to legalize abortion across the country, though it had yet to be passed by the upper house. The Congressional Plaza reverberated with green joy.

During the Senate debate, 143 specialists gave testimony. Belén's case was mentioned. The main spokesperson for the other side was Senator Silvia Elías de Pérez, of Tucumán's ruling party. Another fierce opponent to the bill was Gabriela Michetti, who served as both vice president of Argentina and president of the Senate. The Congressional Plaza once again filled with people, although on this occasion it rained nonstop. This time the result of the vote was different: thirty-eight nays, thirty-one yeas, and two abstentions. The bill to legalize abortion did not pass.

**We come together
and now you see us**

Feminism will triumph, it will triumph.

To be continued . . .

...NEW SEASON: REVENGE

Presidential Elections

President Mauricio Macri, leader of a center-right coalition, is nearing the end of his term and plans to run for reelection. His most prominent opponent seems to be Alberto Fernández, a member of the Justicialist Party founded by Juan Domingo Perón. Fernández's candidacy was put forward by his running mate, former president Cristina Fernández de Kirchner.

As in every presidential election year, Congress enters a recess period. Though it seems like not much is happening, this is far from the truth. A hotbed of coalitions is forming in the struggle for power.

Abortion is relegated to the background, all but vanishing from the political agenda. Polls conducted in 2018, when abortion was last debated in Congress, demonstrate that the issue fails to garner voter support. In fact, it loses voter support. The strongest voices are once again those of the National Campaign for Abortion and the women in the women's decentralized movement—women who, since the massive 2015 #NiUnaMenos march, have learned that any cause that crosses their paths can mobilize thousands in an instant, be it online or in the streets, whether to promote a hashtag or to shake the status quo.

Political leaders in favor of legalizing abortion are faced with the dilemma of political survival and election platforms. If they call for legalizing abortion, they could find themselves sidelined. At the end of the day, conservative political elements tend to be best at securing financial backing, making noise, and using their veto powers.

Before the presidential debates, there are two instances that shed light on where each of the main candidates stands.

At a campaign event in Buenos Aires Province—the largest district in the country and the one with the highest voter turnout in presidential elections—governor María Eugenia Vidal, director of the Republican Proposal (PRO) political party, and Mauricio Macri's best bet for securing reelection, receives a light-blue bandana from a woman in the crowd, a symbol of the "save both lives" movement against abortion. Vidal takes the bandana, raises it, then ties it around her wrist. PRO, which is part of the Juntos por el Cambio coalition (Together for Change), has decided to close ranks with the light-blue movement in this election cycle.

This gesture is counterweighted by an episode few people know about—by decision of those involved. Mere days after Alberto Fernández announces his candidacy, his campaign manager, Santiago Cafiero, receives a phone call from a pro-abortion activist. Over two decades earlier, she'd been fortunate to work with his father, Juan Pablo Cafiero, a former congressman and the leader of a center-left political party that is as illusory in Argentina as it is short lived.

"It's so good you're there. We'd love to speak with Alberto Fernández about an issue we'll be insisting on during the election cycle and after, with whoever becomes president: legalizing abortion."

"I'll talk to him," Santiago replies.

A few days later, Alberto Fernández is admitted to the hospital. The tabloids fear the worst. The presidential candidate's somewhat lackluster communication skills don't help: instead of conveying a calm aura, he telegraphs concerns for his health.

This is where things stand when I receive a phone call one Wednesday in April at eleven a.m.

"Alberto will see you tomorrow."

"But isn't he in the hospital?" I ask.

"Yes, but he's being released and will see you at his house," they reply.

The following day, journalists Ingrid Beck and Noelia Barral Grigera, actress Dolores Fonzi, and I dodge the press and cameras posted around Alberto Fernández's rental apartment in Puerto Madero, and make our approach. I said at the time that the meeting was informal, somewhat random, and unplanned, and I stand by this statement. Plus, only a handful of the thousands of us who'd been working to legalize abortion were able to attend.

We get there at almost the same time as Fernández. We're greeted by Santiago Cafiero and Dylan, a rough collie who's become something of a celebrity.

Our conversation with Alberto Fernández lasts just over an hour. He informs us that his health issues are minor and expresses anger at how journalists have misrepresented his condition. He asks what we want to talk about.

"It's important to us that women's issues be part of your platform. And we won't stop until abortion is legalized," we say.

"Know that I'm your ally," he replies. "As a professor of criminal law, I can't allow women to be prosecuted for choosing not to be mothers." He mentions the Natividad Frías decision. And since he isn't aware of the Belén case, I tell him about it.

"I'm writing a book about her story. As soon as it's published, I'll send you a copy and invite you to the launch."

"Of course," Alberto Fernández replies. "I'll be there."

President Alberta

Election Day has been a holiday in Argentina since democracy was reinstated in 1983.

202 ✹ ANA ELENA CORREA

As predicted, abortion is not a major campaign issue. The more ardent activists are hesitant to put their candidates in a difficult spot. The need to be strategic is either a bane or a boon for the feminist agenda. But in the presidential debate, the issue cannot be avoided. Left-wing candidate Nicolás del Caño is emphatic: Alberto Fernández makes his position clear, as does Mauricio Macri.

The conservative sectors do not use Alberto Fernández's position on abortion against him. Instead, they leak the news that the presidential candidate's only son is a drag queen. They publish pictures from his Instagram account, expose him, call into question the "capability" of a man whose son is a big name on the drag scene. They are horrified at the thought of Fernández taking up residence in Olivos with a son "like that." Fernández tells the press he loves his son.

On election day, Belén is happy to be voting, like countless others across the country. She's excited the book is done and hopeful that a change of guard will bring her more freedom. She feels as if the future might just give her a break.

Preliminary results indicate that the lawyer Alberto Fernández, a seasoned politician with more than thirty years under his belt, will be the next president of Argentina. Former president Cristina Fernández de Kirchner, who still goes by the last name of her late husband, former president Néstor Kirchner, will be vice president of Argentina. A large contingent of Peronistas has appointed her as their undisputed political leader.

Pro-abortion activists are excited when a group of gay people, trans people, and drag queens cheer and chant "President Alberta." But they are worried to see Juan Luis Manzur, the governor of Tucumán, one of the most restrictive provinces for women's rights, invited onstage. They know Manzur was integral to the campaign's victory. They also know that the women's movement and LGBTQIA+ collectives tipped the scale to get Alberto Fernández elected president of Argentina. The next few weeks will tell whose side he is truly on.

The Book Launch

What once seemed impossible becomes reality. *Somos Belén* (*What Happened to Belén*—the original, Spanish-language edition of the book you hold in your hands) will hit shelves before the end of 2019. It's time to plan the launch.

Our narrator sticks her nose back into a story that is not her own—or is, because Belén is so deeply the women of Argentina it hurts.

Back to November 2019. Someone has the idea of launching the book at the University of Buenos Aires' Faculty of Law. There are no small or medium classrooms available, or any reasonably sized assembly halls. November is when the university holds the year's backlog of public classes, ceremonies, and events. Plus, everyone knows December is a bad month for events.

"The only room available is the assembly hall," says Liliana Ronconi of the Faculty of Law's Center for Human Rights.

"Absolutely not," I reply. "There's no way we can fill it. It seats fifteen hundred people."

"We'll fill it."

"We won't."

"We will."

"We won't."

I have two finished copies of *Somos Belén*. On the jacket is a mask like the ones worn by the protestors who marched for Belén's freedom. Like the one she had on as she walked out of prison. Like the imaginary mask she is still wearing. We meet up to enjoy a slice of chocolate and dulce de leche cake. She signs my copy of the book, and I sign hers.

"You know what I was thinking? I want there to be masks at the book launch," Belén says. She laugh-cries when I tell her I had the same idea but didn't have the nerve to say so.

"Can you see if the president can make it to the launch?" Belén asks.

"Of course. But he's probably getting ready to take office, appointing his cabinet, putting together his management agenda. I'll invite him. I just don't know if he'll be able to come. The masks will be easier. I'll get them at a party store, and we can both wear them to the launch."

"Sounds good."

Vilma

Years have passed and a lot has changed in Argentina since Vilma worked as a parliamentary secretary at the Constitutional Reform Convention in 1994. At the time, she advised Broad Front (FG), a center-left political party formed by opponents of Carlos Menem, a Peronist turned representative of the economic right wing. She wasn't spoken about in the media; the spotlight was on the political leader Carlos "Chacho" Álvarez and her brother Aníbal Ibarra, a lawmaker in Buenos Aires who'd go on to become a two-term mayor of the same city. But it was known in the hallways that a number of women were invisibly shouldering the work of negotiating between political parties and drafting some of the most interesting parts of the constitutional reform, the ones tied to modern democracies. One of these women was Vilma Ibarra. Those who heard and saw these women at work knew about all they'd accomplished. But their faces were not the ones visible.

The Argentine quota law, which provides that 30 percent of the list of congressional candidates must be made up of women, certainly made it possible for the faces and voices of many women political leaders gain visibility. Vilma Ibarra's time as a representative was cru-

cial to Argentina becoming the first country in Latin America to legalize same-sex marriage in 2010.

Argentina's subsequent economic and political crises put on
standby several advances in gender issues and dismantled the power
slowly being built by women's political alliances.

Vilma left politics after serving as senator and again as representative. She left behind several laws she'd helped draft, and also a dam-
aged reputation due to her close relationship with certain male public
officials: her brother, the mayor of Buenos Aires; and her boss and
friend Chacho Álvarez, the former vice president of Argentina. One
was impeached, the other resigned. Politics in Argentina and else-
where has a habit of remembering women more for their relationship
to men than for their accomplishments.

She was working at a corporate legal department, far from the media and the hustle and bustle of politics, during the #NiUnaMenos
march that sent over half a million women onto the streets.

"That day, I felt like I'd never be alone in feminism again," she
tells me.

When Alberto Fernández took office, he asked her to be his legal and technical secretary. In other words, his eyes and his signature. Vilma hesitated. She didn't have warm memories of her time
in the public eye. But she'd always been interested in that position.
She thought of the #NiUnaMenos march and the legal changes still
needed to secure women's rights.

"I accept," she told the president-elect.

I'm Sorry

Belén stops by my house, and together we go to the hairdresser. The
book launch will take place at five that evening at the Faculty of Law's
assembly hall. As much as she wants to be there, she still isn't ready
for people to know she's Belén. So she decides to sit with the audience,

once again incognito. Her hairdresser turns out to be from Tucumán. She tells him she's going to a book launch but doesn't say which one.

Two hours earlier, I'd gotten a phone call from Vilma Ibarra. "The president will attend the launch." I don't want to mention it to Belén. What if he doesn't show up?

It's a little before the book launch when we arrive at one of the most majestic halls of the Faculty of Law. The building is over a hundred years old. Agostina, from the National Campaign for Abortion, and Magalí, a close friend who will sit with Belén during the event, help us put green bandanas and masks on every seat, until we run out.

Just as in the movie *Big Fish*—except here there isn't death so much as birth—all the characters involved in the last few years' struggle, as well as those who will continue working to get the law passed, begin filing into the hall: Nelly Minyersky, Soledad Deza, Claudia Piñeiro, Paola Bergallo, Celina De la Rosa, Raquel Asensio, Mariela Belski. All the book's characters are here, as are hundreds of students, feminist activists, future politicians. Several of us onstage know the president may come to the event, so we stall. The audience starts chanting, *"Alerta, alerta, alerta que camina, la lucha feminista por Argentina"* ("Caution, caution, Argentina's feminist struggle is walking").

One of the people presenting the book is actor Gonzalo Heredia, whose soap opera Belén watches every day. Gonzalo reads Margaret Atwood's foreword to this book. Dolores Fonzi reads a note Belén wrote especially for the event.

Claudia Piñeiro prolongs the presentation. This is when Vilma Ibarra and Alberto Fernández walk in. Journalists and audience members begin whispering excitedly. What is the president-elect doing in a sea of white masks and green bandanas? He sits quietly in the front row.

The elated whispering continues after we're done saying everything we'd come to say. Someone, maybe Nelly Minyersky, asks the president to take the stage. Alberto Fernández joins us.

"I'm here because I agree with everything that's been said tonight. I commit to legalizing abortion in Argentina." Applause, hugs, selfies.

Belén had watched the entire launch from the ninth row of the side aisle. She takes a bandana from one of the seats, asks Magalí for a copy of her book, quickly signs it, then asks Julieta, the press's publicist, to take the book to the president, along with the following message: "Tell him I want to speak with him."

I'm given the book and her message onstage.

"President, Belén is in the audience. She says she'd like to speak with you. If you'd rather not, that's OK. I didn't tell her you were coming."

"Of course I'll talk to her," he replies.

Alberto Fernández slips offstage. Meanwhile, Magalí walks Belén up the other aisle so that they both end up in the same back room.

Belén needs no introduction. She goes up to the president and hugs him.

"I'm so sorry about everything you went through. Tell me how I can help," he says.

"I need abortion to be legalized. Only then will I truly feel free. I don't want any more women to go through what I did," Belén says.

"I promise you abortion will be legalized," Alberto says.

The Pandemic

On March 1, the president's speech will mark the start of the legislative year. It's Alberto Fernández's inaugural address to Congress. In it, he announces that in the next ten days he will be presenting a bill to legalize the termination of pregnancies, "making it possible for women to access health care when they choose to have abortions."

It's the first time in the history of Argentina that a president has presented a congressional bill to legalize abortion. The historic demands of feminism and the president's promise to Belén are being taken up by newly minted political forces still in the honeymoon phase of fulfilling campaign pledges. Time is in their favor.

But.

There is always a but.

Just days later, Dr. Tedros Adhanom Ghebreyesus of the World Health Organization makes an announcement: "WHO has been assessing this outbreak around the clock and we are deeply concerned both by the alarming levels of spread and severity, and by the alarming levels of inaction. We have therefore made the assessment that COVID-19 can be characterized as a pandemic."

Restrictions are enacted all over the world. International flights and flight routes are suspended. Strict quarantine measures are adopted across several countries. In-person congressional and parliamentary debates are put on hold. Schools are closed. It's no different in Argentina. These closures encroach on the deadline Alberto Fernández had set for the abortion bill.

"What do we do?" Vilma Ibarra asks him.

"We can't risk the bill not passing. We wait," he replies.

And so weeks go by. There is the first COVID-19 case, the first death, the global vaccine race. Feminist activists don't throw in the towel, but they're busy fighting battles on other fronts: from soup kitchens to the health care system, they're taking on 100 percent of the care. Going to the streets is not an option, because the streets are filled with antivaxxers and people who don't believe in social distancing.

Every so often, there are complaints on social media about some of the feminists who worked the hardest to enact the new abortion law. They're accused of giving up; they haven't, but it's not worth fighting over. COVID-19 cases need to decrease, Congress has to go back to holding in-person sessions.

Belén understands. It's the first time in her life she's had formal work. She's far away from her family again, but this time she knows she's not alone. For the first time since leaving Tucumán, she goes to the doctor. She's no longer afraid.

It Will Be Law

It's November, and with the dip in COVID-19 cases, promising news about vaccines, and the end of social isolation, the moment we women have spent a century waiting for is finally here. The president announces that he will present a congressional bill for the "voluntary termination of pregnancies." Women will no longer have to fear arrest when they have abortions, and whosoever elects to undergo the procedure will be able to access it through their health care provider or at a public health clinic. At the same time, a bill is introduced offering comprehensive care for women who choose motherhood, both throughout their pregnancy and the first one thousand days of their baby's life.

Fernández makes the announcement on Twitter:

> It's always been my belief, and I've said so publicly, that the state should support all gestating people on their path to motherhood. But I also believe it's the state's responsibility to tend to the life and well-being of those who choose to terminate early pregnancies.
>
> Criminalizing abortion has done us no good. Instead, it has paved the way for a worrying number of illegal abortions. Approximately 38,000 women a year are hospitalized for abortions, and 3,000 women have died from abortion complications since democracy was reinstated.
>
> Legal abortions save women's lives and protect their reproductive systems, which are often affected by unsafe abortions.

They do not increase or encourage abortions so much as solve a
public health issue.

As we saw in Mexico City and Uruguay, legal abortions also
lead to fewer abortions and abortion-related deaths. Offering
health coverage also facilitates birth-control access, preventing
unwanted pregnancies.

Congress convenes under strict protocols. Senators and representatives swab before going into session. Committee meetings are held on Zoom, and the number of speakers plummets in comparison with the 2018 debate. Not that much time has passed.

At the debate in the Chamber of Deputies, a lawmaker pulls out Belén's book, the version without this chapter. "I want people to look at this book, to know if they've read this book. *Somos Belén* is about a woman from Tucumán who was held in prison for twenty-nine months for having a miscarriage.

"She had terrible representation, most likely a pro-life lawyer. She was cheated. Thankfully, Soledad Deza, a feminist lawyer, showed up and managed to get her released. I have no doubt that Belén is among the women who are demanding the right to abortion."

He was right. Belén is one of those women.

At six a.m., Vilma Ibarra steps away from the stage where she'd been all night long and goes to the offices of representative Silvia Lospenatto, a leader of the opposing party. They'd met shortly after Alberto Fernández took office, at the apartment of a women's rights activist. Just as they did that night, they talk about both parties' votes. This time, they're both wearing face masks. Silvia practices her speech while Vilma vents her frustration at those who'd promised to vote in favor of abortion only to change their minds in the end. The two women can't hide their excitement or nerves at knowing the issue will be voted on in the next half hour. They apply blush and undereye concealer.

Two hours later, the Chamber of Deputies approves the bill to legalize abortion as well as the one-thousand-day support plan.

A national radio station manages to track down Belén. She agrees to an interview.

"I woke up to a message that the Chamber of Deputies had approved the bill. I think it'll become law because women's suffering is finally out in the open.

"I learned to fight—little by little, and from the bottom. Even though things weren't easy for me when I moved to Buenos Aires, I began rebuilding my life from scratch," she told the journalist who interviewed her. "I never imagined I'd be unjustly imprisoned for three years, for doing nothing. But wounds heal.

"I still have nightmares about the doctors, about sitting across from the judge, about crying in the prison yard."

The Senate session is scheduled for after Christmas. There is renewed incredulity. Barring the three senators from Buenos Aires, the rest always spend the holidays in their home provinces. They're never back between Christmas and New Year's.

On December 28, photographs of senators and their suitcases are published on social media along with the message that they are traveling because *it will be law.*

Tuesday, December 29, is our last chance. If the bill isn't approved now, it's unclear when abortion will be legalized. The issue always gets tabled on election years. We're also about to find out that the pandemic is far from being over.

Unlike two years ago, this time none of the senators denies that women in Argentina have been imprisoned for abortions. This time, there is no question.

Belén's case is mentioned in the Senate, just as it was in the Chamber of Deputies. Senator San Luis Eugenia Catalfamo, who was absent two years ago, says she will be voting in favor of the law. She cites Belén's story as one of her reasons for doing so.

"Not all of us are Belén. Some of us can raise our voices and have the privilege of health care access. Others can afford to become mothers. Others experience the same troubles Belén did but are less fortunate because their cases aren't talked about, and so they are still in prison. Then there are others who aren't here to tell their stories today, because they died trying, during miscarriage," she says.

"This issue moves me. A great deal. I still don't understand how it is that, in the twenty-first century, we women still have to relinquish our independence and our freedom to a society that imposes its way of life on us. Why do we have to be the talk of the town? Why do we have to air our most private decisions?" she asks.

"It's within our power to greenlight this bill," she says a few hours before the vote.

At four a.m., with thirty-eight yeas, twenty-nine nays, and one abstention, the Senate approves a bill enshrining women's right to free, legal, and safe abortions.

Women in face masks and green bandanas cry and cheer in the streets. They'd vowed to keep fighting, and here they are now—they've succeeded.

Belén had fallen asleep with the TV on. She'd had a long day at work, and the heat and exhaustion got the better of her. When she woke up, she was truly free at long last.

ACKNOWLEDGMENTS

There are so many people I want to thank that I should start by apologizing for inadvertently leaving anyone out.

My eternal gratitude to the protagonists of this book, Belén and Soledad. For the fight, for standing up to injustice, for going all in, for making us better. For trusting me.

I owe the fact that I was able to start and finish this book to three people. To Paola Bergallo, who liked the idea behind it, encouraged me to pursue it, appreciated the mission, and showed me great feminist altruism and generosity. To María Moreno, who was so enthusiastic about the idea of the book—of all people!—who coached me, edited my work, taught me, and was patient with my tardiness. And to María Lobo, who cheered me with her friendship, guided me with her knowledge of Tucumán, honored me by reading and commenting on my work, and shared literary laughter and tears with me so soon after we met.

That you are reading this book today is all thanks to Rodolfo González Arzac and Nacho Iraola, who put their trust in me and took a chance on this book when the country and the publishing industry were going through difficult times. Rodolfo and Nacho were both interested in this story and willing to do something about it. Thank you, guys! This English edition would not be possible without the interest and enthusiasm of Gabriella Page-Fort of HarperCollins and the careful translation of Julia Sanches.

I am also enormously grateful to Margaret Atwood. For getting involved in this story and committing to the cause. Her decision to join our fight and write about Belén—and about all of us, because we are all Belén here—was invaluable.

Thank you to Sergio Olguín, Andrés Fidanza, and Juan Becerra for their loving, wise, and stimulating reads.

To our Green Wave, which we call La Minyersky: Ingrid Beck, Noelia Barral Grigera, Claudia Piñeiro, and Leandro Cahn. To our closeness since that year, in this cause and many more. For what we did to make it law.

To Mariela Belski and Paola García Rey, who have been enthusiastic from the beginning. This book is also yours.

To Ariel Zak and Tania.

To Eleonora Lamm, Lourdes Bascary, Silvia Lospennato, and Paola Bergallo, for the trip we took to Santa Marta, Colombia, where I had the idea for this book.

To the NUM girls: Ingrid Beck, Florencia Etcheves, Valeria Sampedro, Marcela Ojeda, Micaela Libson, Marina Abiuso, Hinde Pomeraniec, Mercedes Funes, and Soledad Vallejos. For teaching me so much and because I love you to bits.

To Raquel Asensio, because everything is so connected. For working on the FAL case and the Belén case and for all his teachings.

To Nelly Minyersky, and all the joy and excitement she felt for this book. The Campaign. Her love for Soledad, Belén, and Tucumán. The cause.

To Mariana Carbajal for having given Belén the floor when few wanted to listen to her.

To Magalí Valladares, Julieta Lopérgolo, Jessica Lipinski, Valeria Pegoraro, Liliana Tedeschi, and Vanessa Molinuevo. For all they know and so much more.

To Julieta Correa and Rafaela Correa, for the support and for being there.

To Fernando Torrente. Never underestimate the power of a feminist therapist. Thank you so much.

To Gonzalo Heredia, for being one of the most feminist work colleagues I've ever had.

To Vilma Ibarra, without whom this law would not exist.

To Leticia Cristi, Matías Mosteirin, Dolores Fonzi, and Blas Martínez. For what is coming. To Felicitas Tedeschi, for her courage and coherence.

To Juan Méndez, Celeste Braga Beatove, Fernanda Doz Costa, Sebastián Pisarello, Damián Muñoz, Valeria Foglia, Yanina Muñoz, Bernardo Erlich, Adriana Alvarez, Mariana Romero, Julieta Di Corleto, Larisa Moris, Muriel Santa Ana, Edurne Cárdenas, Victoria Tesoriero, Gabriela Adamo, Gustavo Iglesias, Paula Etchegoyen, Federico Masso, Gabriela Schujman, Mariana Cardelli, Eugenia García, Agustina Ramón Michel, Luciana Peker, Raquel Vivanco, Gisela Busaniche, Malena Pichot, and Flor Sabaté for generously responding to my every query.

To my mother, who taught me to read and who taught me it's possible to both fight and to have empathy.

To Juan Forn, María Moreno, and my third-grade teacher for teaching me how to write.

To the two people who help me get up again and again, who fill my life with light, who teach me so much, and who I love with all my heart. Thank you for all your excitement and for believing in this book even more than me. I hope the world you grow up in sheds many of the injustices that are in this book. To you, Felipe and Malena. Thank you.

Let it be law.

ABOUT THE AUTHOR

Ana Correa is a lawyer, a journalist, and a feminist based in Buenos Aires, Argentina. She has worked with organizations including Amnesty International and was one of the organizers behind the Ni Una Menos women's rights campaign in 2015.

ABOUT THE FOREWORD AUTHOR

Margaret Atwood, whose work has been published in more than forty-five countries, is the author of over fifty books, including fiction, poetry, critical essays, and graphic novels. In addition to *The Handmaid's Tale*, now an award-winning television series, her works include *Cat's Eye*, short-listed for the 1989 Booker Prize; *Alias Grace*, which won the Giller Prize in Canada and the Premio Mondello in Italy; *The Blind Assassin*, winner of the 2000 Booker Prize; The MaddAddam Trilogy; *The Heart Goes Last*; *Hag-Seed*; *The Testaments*, which won the Booker Prize and was long-listed for the Giller Prize; and the poetry collection *Dearly*. She is the recipient of numerous awards, including the Peace Prize of the German Book Trade, the Franz Kafka International Literary Prize, the PEN Center USA Lifetime Achievement Award, and the *Los Angeles Times* Innovator's Award. In 2019 she was made a member of the Order of the Companions of Honour in Great Britain for her services to literature. She lives in Toronto.

ABOUT THE TRANSLATOR

Julia Sanches is a literary translator working from Portuguese, Spanish, and Catalan. Recent translations include *Undiscovered* by Gabriela Wiener, shortlisted for the International Booker Prize in 2024; *Boulder* by Eva Baltasar, shortlisted for the International Booker Prize in 2023; and *Migratory Birds* by Mariana Oliver, for which she won the 2022 PEN translation prize. Born in Brazil, she currently lives in Providence, Rhode Island.